YANKEES IN THE HALL OF FAME

On Memorial Day 1932, a monument, to a man whom *Brooklyn Times Union* sportswriter Bud Nelson called "the most likable character in the sports world" who possessed "an unconquerable spirit," was dedicated in center field at Yankee Stadium. Miller Huggins was joined by Lou Gehrig in 1941 and George Herman "Babe" Ruth in 1949 (pictured here). These memorials laid the foundation for Monument Park, which, in 2023, honors 37 Yankees with six monuments, which are always added posthumously, and 31 memorials. (Courtesy of Raymond Sinibaldi.)

FRONT COVER: Lou Gehrig Day brought over 61,000 fans to Yankee Stadium on July 4, 1939. Mayor LaGuardia opened, calling him "the greatest prototype of sportsmanship and good citizenship." Manager Joe McCarthy spoke, followed by Babe Ruth; after which, MC Sid Mercer said, "Lou has asked me to thank you all for him, he is too moved to speak." The crowd began to chant, "We want Lou," and the Babe then whispered to him, "C'mon kid, buck up now, we're all with you." Gehrig gathered himself and delivered his iconic address. (Courtesy of the National Baseball Hall of Fame.)

COVER BACKGROUND: State-of-the-art Motel T Fords lined the road outside Yankee Stadium on opening day 1923. Christened "the House that Ruth Built," the stadium stood unchanged until 1974. Undergoing a significant renovation during a two-year project brought about the creation of Monument Park beyond center field. Yankee Stadium II stood into the new millennium until Yankee Stadium III was opened right next door to where it all began neigh a century before. (Courtesy of Raymond Sinibaldi.)

BACK COVER: Derek Jeter and Mariano Rivera celebrate their 2009 world championship together on the field of the brand-new Yankee Stadium. They were teammates for 15 seasons and world champions five times. Exceptional postseason performers, they each garnered a World Series MVP award. They became the faces of New York's dynasty as they carried the Yankee tradition into a new "stadium" and a new millennium. No two Yankee careers have been more closely linked than Derek Jeter and Mariano Rivera. (Courtesy of Chris Pedota, the *New York Daily News*.)

YANKEES
IN THE
HALL OF FAME

Kerry Keene, David Hickey, and Raymond Sinibaldi

ARCADIA
PUBLISHING

ISBN 978-1-4671-0993-2

Published by Arcadia Publishing
Charleston, South Carolina

Printed in the United States of America

Library of Congress Control Number: 2023934306

For all general information, please contact Arcadia Publishing:
Telephone 843-853-2070
Fax 843-853-0044
E-mail sales@arcadiapublishing.com
For customer service and orders:
Toll-Free 1-888-313-2665

Visit us on the Internet at www.arcadiapublishing.com

For Rachael, whose unconditional love and unwavering support are never-ending

—David

For Henry Waylon Sinibaldi and Melrose Anne Stoval,
the two latest members of my favorite team

—Raymond

To Pam, whose endless patience allowed me to devote
all the time necessary to a project such as this

—Kerry

CONTENTS

ACKNOWLEDGMENTS

The Society for American Baseball Research (SABR) bio project is a national baseball treasure, and baseballreference.com is a constant source of both information and amazement both were an integral part of this story. Nothing brings a clearer perspective than to read about people and the events they create as they happened; newspapers.com allows that to happen, and for that, we are grateful. Quotes contained herein came from biographies, newspapers, magazines, and previously recorded interviews. The treasure trove that is the National Baseball Hall of Fame website contributed as well. Thanks to Mark Guthrie for his insights and Rachael Adams for hers. And as always Lynda, *sei la mia anima e i miei cuori ispirazione.*

All the photographs of hall of fame plaques were taken by David Hickey. Unless otherwise noted, all the photographs in chapters one and six are from Kerry Keene's personal collection, those in chapters two and five are from David Hickey's personal collection, and the images in chapters three and four are from Raymond Sinibaldi's personal collection.

On June 12, 1939, the baseball world gathered on the lawn outside the new National Baseball Hall of Fame in Cooperstown, New York. The classes of 1936, 1937, 1938, and 1939, comprising 25 men, were inducted. Two were New York Yankees: Babe Ruth and "Wee Willie" Keeler. Babe was one of the five initial electees in 1936, while Keeler was elected in 1939. Lou Gehrig joined the 1939 class in a unanimous vote of the writers in a special December election.

INTRODUCTION

It would surprise a significant number of New York baseball fans to learn that their New York Yankees, undeniably the most successful organization in the long history of American sports, were not part of the original eight franchises that began the American League in 1901. The team replaced the Baltimore franchise, which was dissolved following the new league's second season. By mid-1902, the ownership of the Orioles had fallen into complete disarray, with the situation so dire that league president Ban Johnson seized control of the franchise. Johnson desired to place a team in New York City, seeking local ownership and a suitable place for a ballpark. It was the Ides of March 1903 when the third column of the *New York Times* sports page read, "Home Nine Incorporated," and "The Greater New York Baseball Association was incorporated in Albany yesterday with a capital of $100,000 to operate the American League baseball franchise in this city."

Thirty-eight days later, the New York franchise arrived in the nation's capital to battle the Washington club. Manager Clark Griffith called upon Jack Chesbro to pitch the inaugural game of the New Yorkers' maiden campaign. A record crowd of 11,050 gathered at American League Park as Jack Chesbro took on the Senators. It took an hour and 45 minutes for the Senators to dispose of the New Yorkers by a 3-1 score. The only run they could muster was scored by a fellow named Wee Willie Keeler, a five-foot, four-inch, 140-pound 31-year-old. Lefty swinging outfielder Willie Keeler was an 11-year veteran who defected from the National League, where he had earned the moniker "Hit 'em where they ain't." He became the New York Americans' first star. Chesbro was on the mound again eight days later when 16,243 fans made their way to Hilltop Park for the Highlanders' first home game, a complete-game 6-2 win.

A week before their first game, the *New York Evening World* ran a story suggesting an "appropriate nickname" for the "invading Americans." The suggestion was spun in a playful yarn involving two characters, "the Fat Fan" and the "Elongated Enthusiast." The two were debating whether they should be called the Lowlanders, the Highlanders, or simply the Islanders when a passerby interjected. "You fellows think Griffith's men are going to land near the top don't you?" "Yep," came their swift reply. "Well then," the stranger retorted, "they'll be the Highlanders." A whimsical tale, to be sure, yet the name carried a great source of pride for the highly Scot/Irish population of New York City's highlands. For New York's 79th Highlander Regiment had fought valiantly throughout the Civil War. Named after the queen's Cameron Highlanders of the British Army, they were at Bull Run, Secessionville, Antietam, Fredericksburg, Vicksburg, the Wilderness, Petersburg, and Appomattox, becoming one of New York's most respected fighting units.

For 10 years, they bore that moniker; however, there were not many "near the top" landings for "Griffith's men." The closest they came to a World Series was in 1904 when after a summer-long battle with the Boston Americans, they fell a game and a half short of the pennant. However, the National League champion New York Giants refused to play the upstarts from the new league in what would have been the second World Series. Highlander manager Clark Griffith issued a challenge to "James Collins, manager and captain of Boston's World Champions." In his open letter, which ran in the *New York Journal*, he stated in part, "As the New York Nationals . . . seem unwilling to play ball, the New York Highlanders hereby challenge the Boston's World Champions to a series of games, best three out of five." That challenge did not materialize in 1904, and it took 74 years before the "Bostons" and "New Yorkers" would meet in a postseason "challenge" match, which took place on October 2, 1978, in a one-game winner-take-all event. The New Yorkers prevailed in a win that would catapult them to their 22nd world championship. That championship took place in what could be described as the Yankees' fifth generation, and shortest reign, of excellence and dominance. The generations intertwine and overlap, each connected and characterized by a collection of hall of famers with one or two who were just a cut above the rest.

The first baseball reference to the New York Yankees came in a newswire release on December 7, 1904, out of North Adams, Massachusetts, Jack Chesbro's hometown. It reported that "Happy Jack Chesbro . . . of . . . the New York Yankees . . . had an offer to coach the Harvard pitchers this winter." By 1911, the nicknames were interchangeable, and when their lease on Hilltop Park expired after the 1912 season, they were forced to become tenants of the Giants at the Polo Grounds in Harlem. The following year, the name "Yankees" emerged as the organization's prevailing sobriquet. Whether they be Highlanders or Yankees, what was transpiring on the field did not change, as the New Yorkers continued to lose more than they won. And then, along came George Herman "Babe" Ruth.

Headlines across America screamed the news "Babe Ruth Sold To Yankees," and "Yankees Buy Babe Ruth," and the face of baseball was forever altered. When Babe arrived in 1920, he carried with him back-to-back home run titles, including a new major-league record of 29 in 1919. In his first year in New York, he obliterated his own home run record, with 54 homers, and put up stratospheric offensive numbers the likes of which had never been seen, setting new offensive paradigms that redefined the meaning of power and production. In December 1920, a 21-year-old pitching prospect who was Babe's teammate on the 1919 Red Sox was acquired by the Yankees. Waite Hoyt won 19 games in 1921 as the Yankees landed their first berth in the World Series, in which Hoyt pitched three games (2-1 in 27 innings) and did not surrender an earned run. He pitched in front of Babe in six World Series and joined him in the hall of fame in 1969. In 1923, the Yanks reached the World Series for the third-straight season and, for the third-straight season, faced the New York Giants. However, there were two distinct differences in this "Fall Classic"; one was the "House that Ruth Built" was completed, and Yankee Stadium would host World Series games. The other was an acquisition of another of Babe's former mates from the Red Sox. In January 1923, Herb Pennock, a lanky southpaw, joined the Yankee pitching staff and provided the missing piece. He won two games in the series, including the clincher, and the Yankees claimed their first world championship. Pennock was a part of five Yankee World Series teams, winning 162 games along the way. He pitched in four World Series, never losing a game (5-0), and in 1948 joined Babe in the hall of fame. On June 15 of the Yankees' first world championship season, 20-year-old Lou Gehrig, who had just signed out of Columbia University, replaced Wally Pipp at first base in the ninth inning of a 10-0 win against the St. Louis Browns at Yankee Stadium. He fielded a ground ball and stepped on first to record the game's final out. On June 2, 1925, Gehrig once again replaced Pipp, this time in a start at first base as manager Miller Huggins's attempted to shake the malaise from the Yankee lineup. It worked, as he had three hits and four RBI in a win over the first-place Senators. It was May 2, 1939, before Lou Gehrig came out of the Yankee lineup. Gehrig and Ruth became the greatest three-four combination in baseball history, and they both were inducted into the hall of fame in its inaugural year of 1939.

The concept for the institution designed to honor the great contributors from the game's past was created in 1936, the year after Babe Ruth retired. He was among the first five players tabbed by the baseball writers to receive this honor. Three years later, on June 12, 1939, with the construction of the museum completed, the inaugural induction ceremony was held to formally enshrine Ruth and the 24 others who had been elected between 1936 and 1939. Wee Willie Keeler, the Yankees' original star, was a part of this inaugural class. Gehrig joined the inaugural class of 1939 in December by virtue of a unanimous vote of the baseball writers in a special election.

There are only nine Yankees inducted into Cooperstown who played their entire careers wearing a Yankee uniform; Lou Gehrig was the first. Two others arrived in the Ruth era: outfielder Earle Combs in 1924 and catcher Bill Dickey in 1928.

In 1926, Tony Lazzeri, an Italian kid from San Francisco, made his way to the Bronx and completed what became affectionately known as "Murderers' Row," the first six hitters in the lineup of the 1927 Yankees, one of baseball's most legendary teams. Combs played on four pennant winners and three World Series champs. Dickey was an anchor behind the plate and part of nine World Series, winning eight of them. The Yankee second baseman for 12 seasons, Lazzeri became baseball's first star of Italian descent, participating in six World Series and winning them all. The writers tabbed Dickey for the hall of fame in 1954, while Combs (1970) and Lazzeri (1991) were elected by the Veterans Committee.

The Yankees' second era of excellence and dominance began in 1936 when another Italian kid arrived from San Francisco. Joseph Paul "Joe" DiMaggio played 13 seasons from 1936 to 1951. He was a three-time MVP and an All-Star every year he played. He participated in 10 World Series, of which the Yankees won nine, including an unprecedented four in a row (1936–1939). He took up his rightful place in Cooperstown in 1955. A skinny kid from Queens showed up to play shortstop in DiMaggio's magical season of 1941. Another career Yankee, Phil Rizzuto played 13 seasons, participating in nine World Series, of which the Yankees won seven. He joined DiMaggio in the hall of fame in 1994. Yogi Berra came on board in 1946 and by 1949 was a stalwart behind the dish and became a main cog in the Yankee juggernaut of the 1950s. A three-time MVP and participant in 14 World Series, the writers tabbed him for Cooperstown in 1972. And in 1949, Casey Stengel took the Yankee helm and guided them through the most successful decade of any team in history.

Mickey Charles Mantle was a 19-year-old rookie in Joe DiMaggio's last campaign, and they played in the outfield together in the 1951 World Series, which was the Yankees' third-straight world championship. The Mantle era was ushered in with World Series wins in 1952 and 1953, giving the Yankees an unprecedented five consecutive world championships, a feat that has never been duplicated. A year before Mantle's arrival, Whitey Ford arrived in 1950, and before he was finished, he pitched in 11 World Series in 16 seasons and won more World Series games than any other pitcher in history. Mickey Mantle, who possessed supreme natural skills, became an all-American hero and one of the most iconic, idolized ballplayers of all time. Together, he and Ford became the most potent player/pitcher combo in World Series history, playing in a collective 23 Fall Classics and winning a combined 14 times. Appropriately, the two were ushered into their place in immortality together on the library steps of Cooperstown in 1974.

From 1921 through 1964, the Yankees won 29 American League pennants, and they captured the World Series 20 times. Fourteen pennants and nine world championships came from 1949 through 1964. From their first appearance in a World Series in 1921 through their 29th appearance in 1964, they never went more than four years without winning the pennant, and they had but one losing season, but that all was about to change. The next decade produced drastic changes across the landscape of Major League Baseball (MLB). Divisional play arrived in 1969, and 1974 gave birth to free agency. And for 11 consecutive seasons, the Yankees were mired in mediocrity, never finishing higher than second, and in 1966 suffering a last-place finish for the first time since the Highlanders of 1912.

The pieces that completed the team's return to glory came via free agency. The first came in December 1974 when the Yankees won a bidding war with the Red Sox and landed 1974 Cy Young Award–winner "Catfish" Hunter. They captured the American League (AL) pennant in 1976 but were swept by Cincinnati in the Fall Classic, prompting the team to once again seek strengthening through free agency. This time, they found Reginald Martinez Jackson, Hunter's teammate on three straight Oakland A's world championship teams. With a flamboyant cockiness and panache, he declared himself "the straw that stirs the drink." What followed were back-to-back world championships, which the Yankees had not seen in 15 years. In those two World Series, Jackson hit a combined .419 with seven homers and 16 RBI, cementing his place in Yankee folklore and earning him the nickname "Mr. October." In six seasons (1976–1981), the Yankees reached four World Series and won two of them.

It took 15 years for the Yankees to find their way back to the Fall Classic, the longest stretch since the founding of the franchise. It began with the arrival of two homegrown players: one a pitcher and the other a shortstop. Mariano Rivera and Derek Sanderson Jeter made their major-league debuts just six days apart in May 1995. Like Whitey Ford and Mickey Mantle a half-century before them, they became the linchpins in the Yankees' fifth generation of excellence and dominance. Joe Torre, a 14-year journeyman manager, joined them in 1996, and the three stood on the field in Yankee Stadium that October celebrating the Yankees' first world championship since 1978. The trio shared six American League pennants and four world championships as they became the third generation of Yankees to capture three consecutive World Series. Torre departed, but "the Captain and the Sandman" christened the new Yankee Stadium in 2009 with yet another world championship, the 27th for baseball's most storied franchise. Although retired, the pair were not finished making baseball history. In 2019, Mariano Rivera became the first player ever to garner 100 percent of the writers' vote for induction into the hall of fame. Jeter followed in 2020 capturing 396 of a possible 397 votes.

Since 2000, the Yankees have appeared in postseason play all but four seasons (83 percent of the time). They have won four pennants and two World Series—a record of tremendous success that most franchises would envy. However, the New York Yankees are not most franchises, and as the 2023 season unfolds, they are 14 years removed from their last world championship. Since they won their first World Series in 1923, they have averaged a world championship every four years and an American League pennant every three. There are many in the Bronx thinking that their Yankees are long overdue.

From that initial induction ceremony in 1939 through 2022, fifty-eight players, managers, and executives of the New York Yankees have been immortalized in bronze in the hall of fame's gallery of plaques. Twenty-eight of them are listed on the hall of fame's website with the Yankees as their primary team. Of those 28, only 19 of them are players, and of those 19, only 9 began and ended their careers wearing the iconic Yankee pinstripes. Many past Yankee greats enter into the ongoing discussion of the hall of fame, and many are indeed worthy. Their future lay in the hands of the hall of fame era committees. This is the story of those Yankees who rest in perpetual glory in Cooperstown's hallowed halls.

1

ONCE UPON A HILLTOP

On April 30, 1903, the New York Americans played their first game at Hilltop Park. "To the American League's long hard fight to establish a baseball club in this city, there came a climax yesterday," wrote the *New York Sun*. "The first game in New York of that young and powerful organization was played on the new park in Washington Heights." That "young and powerful organization" soared to heights that none could have dared dream. (Library of Congress.)

While the storied New York American League baseball franchise has featured many great and accomplished field managers in its long history, it was Clark Griffith who held the position for its first several years. Not only did he manage the new team for five-and-a-half seasons, but he continued his long and impressive pitching career as well, appearing in 87 games for the Highlanders. Known as the "Old Fox" due to his masterful control on the mound, Griffith had won more than 20 games a season in six different seasons in the 1890s with Chicago of the National League. He played a role in the formation of the American League in 1901 and managed the Chicago White Sox as they captured the league's first pennant. When Ban Johnson came calling in 1903, Griffith became player/manager of the American League's newly formed New York club. He was elected in 1946.

In 1903, when the 33-year-old Griffith came to New York, the hall of fame was years away from being created. Little did the young manager know that he, along with two others from that team, would eventually become baseball immortals. In 1939, Wee Willie Keeler became one of the first Yankee players inducted into the newly created shrine, and in 1946, Griffith himself was inducted alongside Jack Chesbro. (Boston Public Library.)

Wee Willie Keeler made headlines when he officially joined the American League's newly formed New York Highlanders team in 1903. It was considered a coup for New York to start off with a player of Keeler's caliber, earning them instant credibility, and they made him the highest-paid player in the league at $10,000 per year. The two-time batting champion hit over .300 for 17 consecutive seasons. Keeler was elected in 1939.

The diminutive Keeler, who stood just five feet, four inches tall and weighed a mere 140 pounds, was one of the game's most effective hitters because of his ability to "hit 'em where they ain't." His 29-ounce, 30-inch bat is the smallest in major league history, but with it, he displayed great bat control, place-hitting ability, and expert bunting, becoming known as the "King of the Place-Hitters." (Library of Congress.)

Keeler, with his lofty .377 career batting average, immediately became the face of the franchise and its first superstar. On April 22, the franchise's first official game, he became the first player to reach base and score a run in Yankees' history, and eight days later, he became the first to get a hit and score a run at their home field, Hilltop Park. In 1909, he was the last original Yankee on the roster.

Jack Chesbro was the first great New York Yankee pitcher. Little did he know that Cooperstown, New York, a small village roughly 100 miles from his hometown of North Adams, Massachusetts, would play such a significant role in his life. Chesbro, who had pitched with a semipro team in Cooperstown in 1895, made it back permanently a half-century later with his election in 1946.

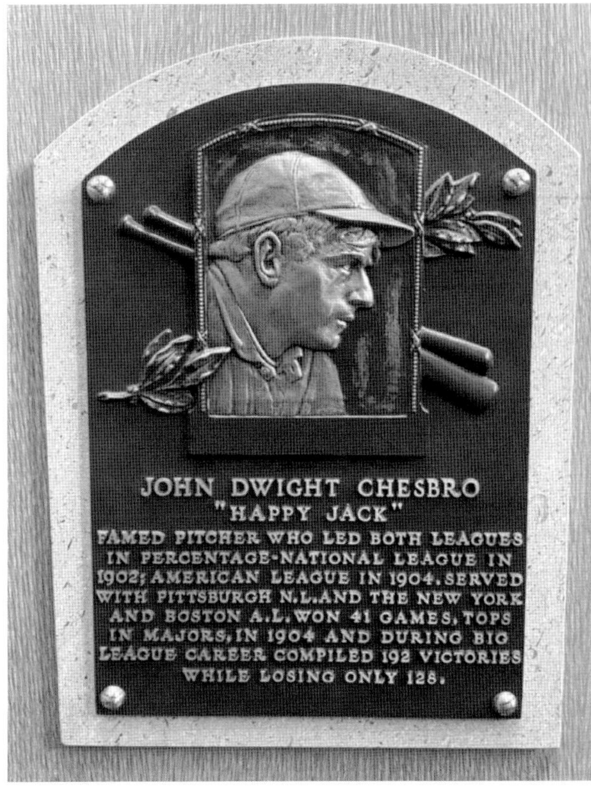

"Happy Jack" Chesbro made his debut with Pittsburgh in 1899, helping them to pennants in 1901 and 1902. He jumped to the newly created New York team in their inaugural season of 1903, starting the first game in franchise history as well as their first home opener. Over a century after his record-setting 1904 season, it remains indelibly etched into baseball history. His 41 victories and 48 complete games are records which will never be broken. (Library of Congress.)

Happy Jack Chesbro's historic 1904 campaign also proved haunting. New York trailed Boston by a half-game, and they ended the season facing off, playing five games in three days. Chesbro started three of those games, winning the first one to put New York into first place and losing the next. The season came down to the last day with New York having to sweep a doubleheader. In a 2-2 game, he uncorked a wild pitch in the ninth inning, allowing the pennant-winning run to score for Boston.

Unfortunately for Branch Rickey but fortunately for baseball, he struggled on the diamond, left baseball, and enrolled in law school at the University of Michigan. Returning in 1914, he managed for 10 seasons before finding his calling as a hall of fame baseball executive, innovator, and pioneer. His "noble experiment," bringing Jackie Robinson to Brooklyn, transformed not only baseball, but America. Rickey was elected in 1967.

Forty years before his historic hiring of Jackie Robinson, Branch Rickey was a 25-year-old catcher with the Highlanders. When New York acquired Rickey from the St. Louis Browns in February 1907, they no doubt recalled how well he played against them the season before. The previous August 6, Rickey slugged two homers—the first off Highlander ace Jack Chesbro and the latter an inside-the-park version. He hit a total of three career homers.

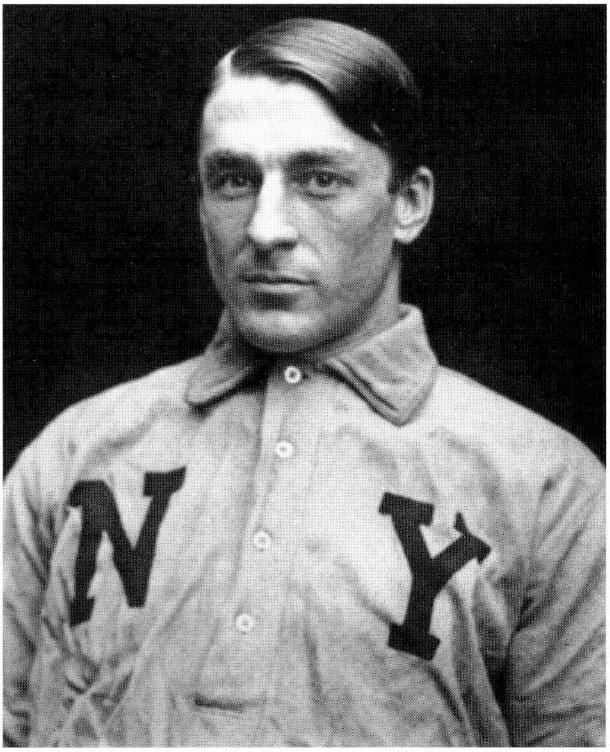

It was a major coup for the American League and New York when the Yankees hired Frank Chance as player/manager in 1913. In seven seasons as the Cubs manager, Chance and the Cubs reached the World Series four times in five years and captured world championships in 1907 and 1908. Yankee fans' initial excitement turned to disappointment as 1913 was one of the worst years (94 losses) in franchise history. Chance resigned in September 1914. He was elected in 1946.

Chance gained fame as the Cubs' first baseman of the double-play combination, which included shortstop Joe Tinker and second baseman Johnny Evers. Written by columnist Franklin Pierce Adams, a poem lamented how often the New York Giants were squelched by a Cubs double play. It read in part, "These are the saddest of possible words, Tinker to Evers to Chance. . . . Ruthlessly pricking our gonfalon bubble, Making a Giant hit into a double, Words that are heavy with nothing but trouble, Tinker to Evers to Chance."

Like many who went on to tremendous managerial careers, Bill "Deacon" McKechnie played under highly accomplished and influential field bosses early in his playing career, including the highly respected Frank Chance in the 1913 Yankee campaign. Chance recognized McKechnie's baseball intelligence and said of him that season, "He's the only man on the club who knows what baseball is all about." Elected in 1962, he was Babe Ruth's last manager.

A journeyman infielder, Bill McKechnie (back row, second from left) achieved a modicum of managerial success with Newark in the Federal League in 1915. Called a "master handler of men," the Deacon was known for creating teams that were consistently better than the sum of their individual parts. In 1922, he began a 24-season managerial career, becoming the first skipper to lead three different franchises to the Fall Classic and the first to win World Series titles with two different teams.

New York City native and businessman Jacob Ruppert Jr. was raised in, and eventually owned, his father's brewery business. A natural leader, Ruppert Jr. was a National Guard colonel and served as a US congressman from 1899 to 1907. His crown jewel was purchasing the New York Yankees for $480,000 in 1915 and turning them into a dynasty. He was elected in 2013.

During his tenure, Jacob Ruppert Jr. (right) acquired 20 future hall of famers, including Babe Ruth, Lou Gehrig, and Joe DiMaggio. The purchase of Ruth (left) and the hiring of Ed Barrow (center) to manage the front office in 1920 launched the team to unprecedented success. Ruppert bought out partner Tillinghast Huston in 1922, and under his reign, the Yankees won 10 pennants and seven world championships.

Citing his "perfect confidence in the future of baseball," Ruppert's Yankees broke ground for a new 70,000-seat stadium on May 5, 1922. Built for $2.5 million, Yankee Stadium opened on April 18, 1923, with double the capacity of the Polo Grounds. It proved a perfect fit, as the Yankees won their first World Series against their former landlords, while drawing 33 percent more fans to their new park during the "Subway Series." (Library of Congress.)

The New York Yankees purchased 24-year-old Charles Arthur "Dazzy" Vance from the Pittsburgh Pirates in 1915. Vance threw 28 innings for New York in 1915 with minimal success. Spending 1916 and 1917 in the minors, the Yankees called him back for another shot in 1918, which proved disastrous, resulting in only two and one-third innings, nine hits, and five runs. Knocking around the minor leagues battling a chronically injured pitching elbow, Vance found himself in Shreveport, Louisiana, in 1920 where, during a friendly poker game, he banged his elbow on the wall while raking in winnings off the table. This ultimately led to surgery that removed bone chips, and Dazzy Vance was reborn. Joining the Dodgers in 1922, the 31-year-old rookie embarked on a career that took him to Cooperstown, where he and Joe DiMaggio were enshrined together in 1955.

Raised on a farm on Maryland's eastern shore, Frank Baker developed powerful arms and hands. In an era when home runs were few and far between, he earned his nickname "Home Run" by slugging round-trippers in back-to-back games, propelling the Athletics to victory in the 1911 World Series. Swinging a 54-ounce bat, he became the first major leaguer in the 20th century to lead his league in homers for four consecutive years. Baker was elected in 1955.

A distant relative of Robert E. Lee, Baker missed the 1915 season due to a contract dispute with Philadelphia and was purchased by New York in February 1916. The Yankees' regular third baseman for five seasons, "Home Run" is considered his era's top-third sacker. The death of his wife in 1920 caused him to sit out the season, but he rejoined the team in 1921 and 1922, the Yankees' first two pennant seasons.

It is a bit ironic that the only position player from the 1921 and 1922 pennant-winning Yankees to make it to Cooperstown, other than Frank "Home Run" Baker, is none other than George "Babe" Ruth. Baker had earned his moniker a few years before Ruth's home run prowess redefined the game. In his 13-year career, Baker never played a single inning anywhere except third base. Including the World Series, the pair combined for 828 homers. Ironically, only 99 were hit by the man they called "Home Run."

As he had done 15 years previously, AL president Ban Johnson suggested a manager for the Yankees 1918 season. New York had become a revolving door with eight managers over the previous 10 years. The five-foot, six-inch, 140-pound Miller Huggins provided much-needed stability. In 12 seasons managing New York, "Mighty Mite" won six American League pennants and three world championships. He was elected in 1964.

In 1918, Huggins took over a Yankees team that had finished no higher than fourth place since 1910. However, by 1921, under the new manager's guidance, a baseball dynasty began to unfold. The next eight years found the Yankees in six World Series, winning three of them. His 1927 Murderers' Row team, loaded with six future hall of fame players is, considered by many, the greatest team in baseball history.

In September 1929, Huggins passed away, succumbing to a blood infection. Through tears, Babe Ruth said, "Nothing I say can express what I feel at the loss of Huggins. . . . He was the only man who knew how to keep me in line." Huggins garnered as much reverence and respect as any man in the game; perhaps best said by Earl Combs, "Huggins was a rare combination of almost all of the virtues and very few of the vices."

2

THE SULTAN ARRIVES

As a young child, George Herman Ruth Jr. roamed the streets of Baltimore until he landed in the St. Mary's Industrial School for Boys at the age of seven. When he was a rookie pitcher in 1915, the *Boston Post* wrote that he was "one of the best natural sluggers ever in the game." He was one of the best left-handed pitchers in baseball in 1918 when his conversion to a position player began, and in 1919, he set a new home run record. In January 1920, Jake Rupert purchased Babe's contract from the Red Sox for the royal sum of $125,000 and added a $300,000 loan, using Fenway Park as collateral. (A total of $6,293,633.75 in 2022 dollars.) They called him "Colossus," "Caveman" and the "Mauler." His remarkable accomplishments, notwithstanding baseball and the New York Yankees, were on the verge of an unimaginable transformation. The "Sultan" had arrived.

When he arrived in New York in 1920, Babe Ruth had already displaced Ty Cobb as the game's number-one drawing card. In his 15 years in New York, he led the team to seven AL pennants and four world championships, laying the foundation for Yankee dynasties to follow. He was among the first five players elected to the hall of fame in 1936 and a member of the inaugural class inducted in 1939.

Babe led the AL a collective total of 85 times in nine offensive categories, including home runs (12), slugging percentage (13), on-base percentage (13), and on-base plus slugging (OPS, 13). When he died, he held 54 MLB records, 10 AL records, and 24 Word Series records. The record of which he was most proud was his 29 2/3 consecutive World Series innings pitched without giving up a run, a record he held until 1961.

On August 11, 1920, Babe Ruth had 41 home runs, 12 more than his record-setting 29 of the previous year. Grantland Rice wrote of Ruth as the living embodiment of Horatio Alger's fictional heroes, "He lured thousands from their happy or sodden homes to see a baseball hoisted out of the lot. . . . None of Mr. Alger's heroes was ever followed by vast mobs and acclaimed almost daily in striking headlines across the front page. . . . Thus does Babe Ruth arise superior to fiction." He finished 1920 with an astounding 54 home runs. In 1921, he "hoisted" 59 "out of the lot" and set a new RBI record. His record-shattering performances led to the construction of Yankee Stadium, which opened in 1923 (above). In 1927, he reset his mark with 60 homers, and on July 13, 1934, he hit home run No. 700 (right) in Detroit's Navin Field.

Following Babe's third consecutive home run record-breaking season (1921), a team of "ivory hunting" scientists at Columbia University did a barrage of tests to find out what made him tick. Hugh Fullerton wrote of their findings, "His eyes and ears function more rapidly than those of other players . . . his brain records sensations more quickly and transmits its orders to the muscles much faster than does that of the average man." In short, he was Superman.

In the last year of his life, Babe established the Babe Ruth Foundation to fight juvenile delinquency and collaborated with journalist Bob Considine on *The Babe Ruth Story*. His dedication read, "This book, the only authentic story of my life, is sincerely dedicated to the kids of America." Babe never forgot his roots, and he never passed up an opportunity to visit kids in orphanages in Boston, New York, Los Angeles, or any city in the country.

While sitting in his apartment wearing his favorite smoking jacket, Babe literally signed thousands of baseballs for hundreds of causes. Contests and competitions were held nationwide to which he lent his name, often with autographed baseballs as prizes. Note that the left-handed pitcher and left-handed swinger is signing right-handed, a definite carryover from his learning to write at St. Mary's.

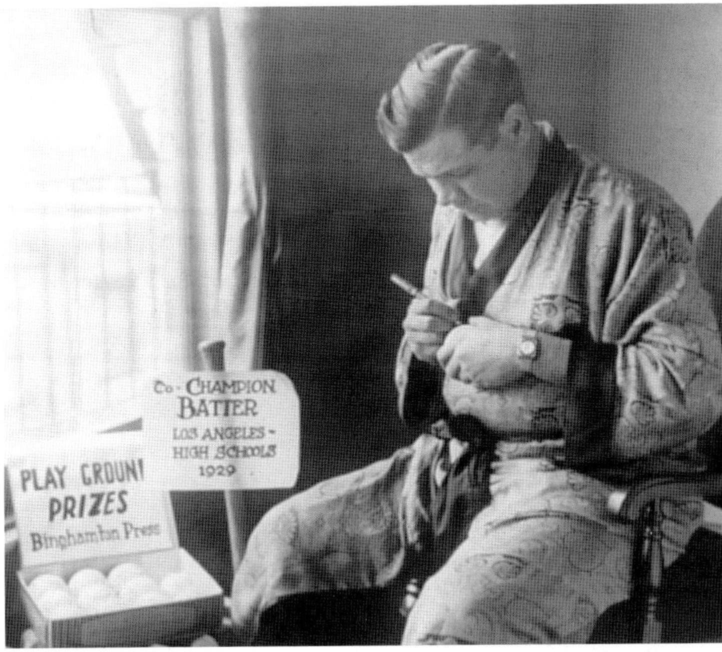

Most of the film footage of Babe was taken later in his career, a potbellied older fella on spindly legs circling the bases. However, he had five seasons in which he had double-digit stolen base numbers, including 10 when he was 35 years old. At six feet, two inches and 195 pounds, he truly was a physically athletic specimen as a younger player.

Lou Gehrig greets Babe at home plate following his 50th home run in 1927. In 1928, he hit 54, his fourth season with 50 or more. Ralph Kiner, Mickey Mantle, and Willie Mays each had two 50-plus homer seasons. It would take until the turn of the 20th century in the throes of the "Steroid Era" for Mark McGwire and Sammy Sosa to join the Sultan with four 50-plus home run seasons.

Babe's coffin laid in Yankee Stadium's lobby, 200 feet behind home plate from where he launched 262 home runs. Over 100,000 people passed his bier, and over 6,000 gathered in St. Patrick's Cathedral for his funeral while another 75,000-plus lined the streets outside. Thousands made their way to Gate of Heaven Cemetery, in the rain, as "the Great Bambino," "the Sultan of Swat," was laid to rest. Grantland Rice wrote, "No game shall ever see his like again."

In June 1920, Robert Ripley inked a cartoon proclaiming Babe "the Sultan of Swat." In August 1948, newspapers across the country chronicled the last days and funeral of the Babe, and in 1956, Mickey Mantle received the first Babe Ruth Sultan of Swat Award. To this day, baseball cards of "Babe Ruth, Sultan of Swat" appear in packs; he took the title with him.

By the time Ed Barrow moved into the Yankees' front office to assume general manager duties, his wealth of experience in pro-baseball management was second to none. He had owned and operated minor-league teams as early as 1894; managed the Detroit Tigers for two seasons (1903–1904); was president of two minor leagues, including the International League from 1911 to 1917; and led the Boston Red Sox to a world championship in 1918. He was elected in 1953.

By late 1920, Barrow (left) departed a Boston team quickly on the decline and joined a Yankee team on the verge of greatness. Barrow had the good fortune to work for Jacob Ruppert (right), who was determined to bring a title to his home city and gave him the resources needed for success. The die was cast and Barrow delivered, as the Yankees captured their first world championship in 1923.

Ed Barrow was born in a covered wagon in Springfield, Illinois, in 1868. The simple country boy's career in baseball started as a concessionaire and ended as a 10 percent shareholder and chairman of the board of the New York Yankees, the greatest sports franchise of all time. He was one of the first executives to put numbers on uniforms, and he retired baseball's first as well, when Lou Gehrig's No. 4 was so honored in 1939.

Twenty-one-year-old pitcher Waite Hoyt truly hit the jackpot when he was traded from the Red Sox, along with three members of Boston's 1918 world championship team, to the Yankees in December 1920. He spent 10 seasons in New York becoming a part of the first magical Yankee dynasty. He was the ace of the pitching staff of the 1927 Murderers' Row squad, leading the league in wins. He was elected in 1969.

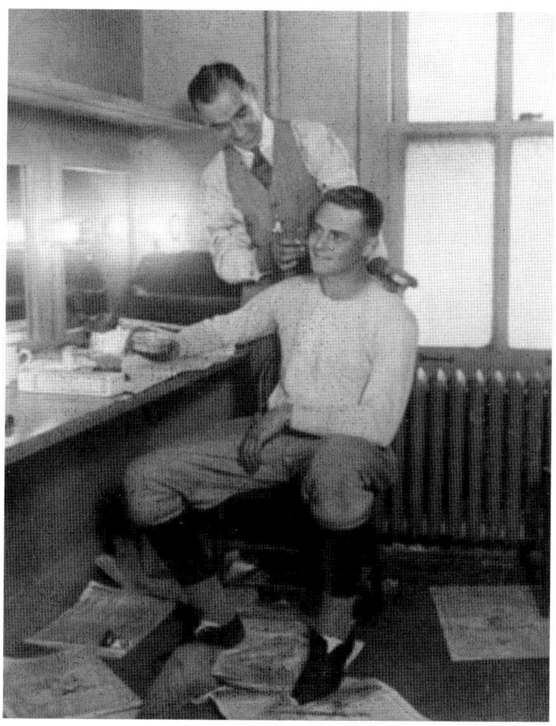

Making his professional debut at 16 earned him the nickname "Schoolboy," and he reached the majors two years later with the Giants. Hoyt impressed manager Miller Huggins enough to give him a regular spot in the starting rotation in 1921. Four complete-game victories in a 13-day span in May led to his 19 wins and helped the Yankees win their first pennant, securing a trip to the World Series.

In the 1921 World Series, Waite Hoyt pitched 27 consecutive innings without allowing an earned run, but only went 2-1 as an infield error in the final game cost him the win and the Yankees the championship. Hoyt went 22-7 in 1927 and 23-7 in 1928, leading the Yankees to back-to-back World Series titles. He made 11 relief appearances in 1928, earning eight saves, which led the American League.

In January 1923, left-handed pitcher Herb Pennock became the 14th and last Red Sox player who had played with Babe Ruth in Boston to be traded to the Yankees. Going from last place to first, Pennock and his wife reportedly broke into a spontaneous dance of joy upon hearing the news. The Yankees would be getting the high-quality starter they truly needed. He was elected shortly after his passing in 1948.

Herb Pennock had a very graceful, seemingly effortless delivery, relying primarily on curves and breaking pitches. As a member of the 1923 team that opened the brand-new Yankee Stadium, Pennock got off to a great start with a 6-0 record by the end of May. His 19-6 record and league-leading .760 winning percentage helped New York win their third-straight American League pennant and first world championship.

Pennock's first season with New York culminated in a terrific performance in the World Series. A complete-game victory in game two, a save securing the victory in game four, and the clinching win in game six ensured his place on the Yankees' staff, which he held for a decade. In his 11 seasons with the team, Pennock's win-loss record was 162-90 (.643) and 5-0 in four World Series.

A graduate of Eastern Kentucky University, Earle Combs became a schoolteacher before opting for baseball. He chose wisely, as he was soon starring for Louisville of the American Association. He joined the Yankees in 1924, and for a decade, he was one of the most popular, well-liked players on the team. Quiet, modest, and deeply religious, "the Kentucky Colonel" quickly became a fan favorite. The Babe said of him, "Combs was more than a grand ballplayer, he was always a first-class gentleman . . . all man and a great competitor." The leadoff hitter of the famed 1927 Murderers' Row lineup, his outstanding on-base percentage (OBP) made him the prototypical table setter for Ruth and Gehrig. Earle (below, second from left) was the starting center fielder on four Yankee pennant winners and three world championship teams. In 1929, Combs was the first Yankee to step to the plate wearing a uniform number on his back—the No. 1 because he was, after all, leading off. He was elected in 1970.

In 1925, Combs's first full season, he had the highest batting average (.342) among all Yankee regulars while leading the team in hits (203) and runs scored (117). His 231 hits, in their legendary 1927 season, remained a team record until surpassed by Don Mattingly in 1986. Combs excelled in four World Series with New York, accumulating an astounding .451 OBP, 9 RBI, and 17 runs scored in 16 games.

In late July 1934, disaster struck 35-year-old Combs while playing in St. Louis. Chasing a fly ball, Combs collided with the outfield wall and fractured his skull. He spent two months in the hospital and was able to return for the 1935 season, although he never regained his old form. Combs retired as a player and served as a Yankee coach from 1936 through 1944.

In 1925, twenty-one-year-old Pacific Coast League (PCL) infielder Tony Lazzeri caught the eye of Ed Barrow and Yankee management. Playing for Salt Lake City, Lazzeri scored 202 runs, had 222 RBI, and set a pro-baseball record with 60 home runs, albeit in a 197-game schedule. Although Lazzeri suffered from epilepsy, the Yankees decided to take a chance and acquired him for $50,000 and three players. Manager Huggins was impressed enough in spring training to name the young San Franciscan his starting second baseman in 1926. He had a fine rookie season, playing every game, and was second to Babe Ruth with 117 RBI. Teammate Frank Crosetti said of Lazzeri that he "not only was a great ballplayer, he was a great man. He was a leader. He was like a manager on the field." Lazzeri was elected in 1991.

Tony Lazzeri's outstanding rookie season was somewhat overshadowed, as he was haunted by his last at bat of the 1926 World Series. He came to bat with the bases loaded in the seventh inning of game seven with two outs and the Yankees trailing 3-2. He nearly became the hero when he hit a ball over the left field fence, but it was just a foul. On the next pitch, the great Pete Alexander struck him out.

Following the 1926 World Series loss, Tony Lazzeri and the Yankees bounced back with championships in 1927, 1928, 1932, 1936, and 1937. On May 24, 1936, Lazzeri had a game for the ages, becoming the first major leaguer to hit two grand slams in one game. In that same game, he also hit a solo homer and a triple and drove in 11 runs, an American League record that still stands. Lazzeri was MLB's first star of Italian descent.

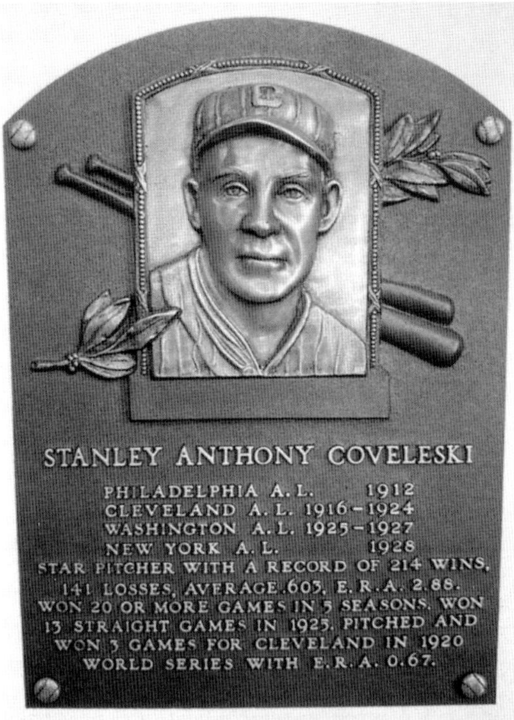

Although the mighty 1927 New York Yankees easily won the pennant and the World Series, they aimed to stay on top and signed veteran star pitcher Stan Coveleski for the 1928 season. The right-hander, who had won 20 or more games five times and was arguably the league's top hurler in 1925, pitched his last 58 innings in pinstripes. Coveleski made his Yankee debut on May 2, 1928, pitching two hitless innings in relief against his old Washington team. Four days later, he got his first start and first Yankee victory. A few weeks later, Coveleski got complete-game wins in back-to-back starts. His 215th and final major-league victory came versus Boston on June 30, 1928, as he beat fellow future hall-of-famer Red Ruffing. Coveleski was inducted in 1969 along with his 1928 teammate Yankee pitcher Waite Hoyt.

When 20-year-old Leo Durocher first donned Yankee pinstripes late in the 1925 season, it was the start of six decades in a major-league uniform. Purchased by New York from Hartford of the Eastern League, he saw his first action in the final two games of 1925. Durocher spent the next two years back in the minor leagues but won the Yankees starting second base job in the spring of 1928. In two full seasons with the Yankees, he split time between second base and shortstop. When New York began wearing uniform numbers in 1929, Durocher sported the No. 7, later made famous by Mickey Mantle. Although not an imposing hitter, his intensity, competitiveness, scrappy play, and tremendous effort were surpassed by very few. Durocher coined the phrase "nice guys finish last," hated losing, and would do anything to win. He was elected in 1994.

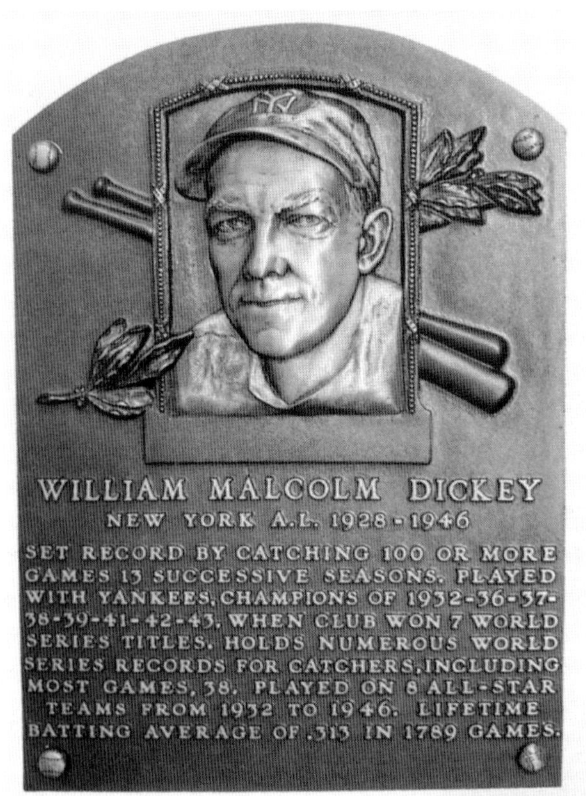

Bill Dickey made his debut late in 1928 and became the starting catcher two weeks into the 1929 season. Joining a lineup replete with four hall of famers, young Dickey fit right in, batting .324 in his rookie campaign while throwing out 50 percent of potential base stealers (20 percent over the league average). It was the first of 11 seasons in which he batted over .300. An 11-time All-Star, Dickey became a perennial MVP candidate and one of the Yankees early all-time greats. He was elected in 1954.

"If this boy doesn't make it, I'll give up scouting," Yankee scout Johnny Nee told the Yankee brass after watching 19-year-old Bill Dickey playing for the Little Rock Travelers in the Southern Association. On the scout's recommendation, the Yankees purchased Dickey from the Jackson Senators for $12,000, and the catcher spent the next 15 years revealing Nee's wisdom.

Following a fine rookie season in 1929, Dickey continued to establish himself as a star both with the bat and behind the plate. In the early 1930s, he emerged as the premier catcher in the American League, supplanting Philadelphia hall-of-famer Mickey Cochrane. A perennial MVP candidate, he was named to the first American League All-Star squad in 1933, and he represented the Yankees in nine of the first 10 "Midsummer Classics."

The exceptional hitting ability Bill Dickey displayed during his first several seasons reached a higher level in 1936. Recording his highest batting average (.362) along with career highs in on-base and slugging percentages, he embarked on a four-season span in which he averaged .326 with 26 home runs and 115 RBI while throwing out 48 percent of runners attempting to steal. It is no coincidence the Yankees won the World Series each year.

In the 1934 season, southern-born-and-bred Bill Dickey and New York City native Lou Gehrig became roommates. Although they came from vastly different backgrounds, these two highly respected gentlemen got along tremendously well and shared many of the same interests. Dickey was the only active Yankee player to appear in the 1942 movie *The Pride of the Yankees*, starring Gary Cooper (above), which chronicled Gehrig's life and premature death in 1941.

As a teenager in Illinois, Ruffing was a good-hitting outfielder until he lost four toes on his left foot in a mining accident. With seriously impaired running ability, the redhead switched to pitching and went on to make his debut with the Red Sox at 19 years old. Fifteen years later, he was the top pitcher on a Yankees team that won its fourth-straight world championship.

When Jacob Ruppert acquired right-handed pitcher Charles "Red" Ruffing early in 1930, he brought with him a career win-loss record of 36-96 in his six-plus major-league seasons. In those years spent with the Boston Red Sox, his team finished in last place five times and next to last once. With New York, Ruffing's fortunes flipped immediately, and by the end of June, he had a record of 6-0. He benefitted from the potent bats of Ruth, Gehrig, Lazzeri, Combs, and catcher Bill Dickey, who also provided outstanding work as Ruffing's batterymate. Ruffing became a mainstay in the Yankees rotation for 15 seasons, saving many of his finer performances for the World Series. The epitome of a big game pitcher, the six-time world champion had a record of 7-2 with a 2.72 earned run average in 10 Fall Classic games. He was elected in 1967.

Red Ruffing was an exceptional hitter in addition to his tremendous pitching ability. In 1932, he threw a complete-game shutout and hit a 10th-inning home run to give the Yankees a 1-0 win against the Washington Senators. In 1935, he led the Yankees in both wins (16) and batting average (.339). Hall-of-fame slugger Jimmie Foxx once said, "That Ruffing is a wonder, always in there winning that important game for you."

Signed by the Yankees in 1931, Joe Sewell hit .302, scored 102 runs, and was assigned to be Lou Gehrig's roommate. In New York's victorious 1932 World Series, he compiled a .333 average and .500 on-base percentage. Remarkably, he struck out only 15 times in 1,753 plate appearances in three seasons with the Yankees. Sewell was elected in 1977.

In August 1920, Cleveland called Joe Sewell up to the majors after only 92 minor-league games. He replaced Ray Chapman, who was struck by a pitch from Carl Mays and later tragically died. Sewell helped Cleveland win the World Series a few months later and became the premier shortstop in the American League in the 1920s. The five-foot, six-inch, 155-pounder used the same bat throughout his entire 14-year career, a 40-ouncer he called "Black Betsy."

Vernon "Lefty" Gomez was a truly colorful character with the Yankees of the 1930s. Well-known for his witticisms and oftentimes self-deprecating quotes, he often said, "I'd rather be lucky than good." In truth, the talented left-hander did not need luck. Born in Northern California, he won 18 games at 20 years of age hurling for San Francisco in the Pacific Coast League. Impressed by his blazing fastball and tremendous curve, the Yankees purchased him in late 1929. Lefty was elected in 1972.

Concerned about him carrying only 145 pounds on his six-foot, two-inch frame, management put him on a program to add weight. Gomez split 1930 between the big club and the minors, and by 1931, he had beefed up to 175 pounds and was in the majors to stay. A four-time 20-game winner, he led the league in strikeouts three times and was 6-0 (in seven starts) in World Series competition. Gomez followed up his 1931 twenty-one-win breakout season with 24 victories in 1932, leading the Yankees to 107 wins on the way to his first World Series. He started game two versus the Chicago Cubs in front of 50,000-plus fans at Yankee Stadium and surrendered only one run in a complete-game victory. New York swept the Cubs, and the 23 year old had the first of his six world championships.

Lou Gehrig (left) and Lefty Gomez (No. 11) combine to nail an opposing runner. The pair played 10 years together, winning five pennants and five world championships. They were All-Star teammates the first seven years of the game's existence, and Gomez not only was the winning pitcher of the first Midsummer Classic ever played, but he drove in the first run in the history of the game as well.

Lefty Gomez and Red Ruffing are arguably the greatest lefty/right pitching combo in Yankee history. In 11 seasons (1931–1941), they combined for eight 20-plus win seasons and 10 All-Star appearances and collectively went 388-210 for a .638 winning percentage. They were equally as masterful in the fall, winning six world championships while going a collective 13-2 in a total of 17 starts.

Joe McCarthy is the most highly accomplished manager to have never played in Major League Baseball. A broken kneecap hampered his development, and McCarthy spent 15 seasons in the minor leagues. He honed his managerial skills with Louisville of the American Association before reaching the big leagues as manager of the Cubs in 1926. He took over a mediocre team and in 1929 led the team to its first pennant in 11 years. With four games left in the 1930 campaign, McCarthy resigned his post when owner Bill Wrigley informed him Rogers Hornsby would replace him for the 1931 season. Amidst allegations of Hornsby's "indifference and . . . veiled insubordination" throughout the season, McCarthy felt it in "the best interest of all involved" to resign. Two weeks later, he signed a two-year deal with the Yankees, and the *Brooklyn Eagle* called him "the most dominant figure to ever run a Ruppert team." Another writer offered, "The coming of McCarthy to New York is one of the biggest achievements of the American League."

Joe McCarthy inherited a team featuring Ruth and Gehrig, and in 1932, he became the first manager to win a pennant in both leagues. He gained sweet revenge with the sweep of the Cubs in the World Series. He managed the Yankees to eight pennants and seven World Series titles, including four in a row from 1936 through 1939. The *Sporting News* wrote, "His ballplayers play the part of champions at all times." His success was truly historic, prompting his election in 1957.

Although soft-spoken, Joe McCarthy (left) was a very confident and well-respected leader. He was the driving force behind the Yankee success in the 1930s and early 1940s. He piloted the transition from the glory days of Ruth and Gehrig to the success of up-and-coming younger stars Joe DiMaggio, Joe Gordon, and Phil Rizzuto. DiMaggio affectionately opined that "never a day went by when you didn't learn something from Joe McCarthy."

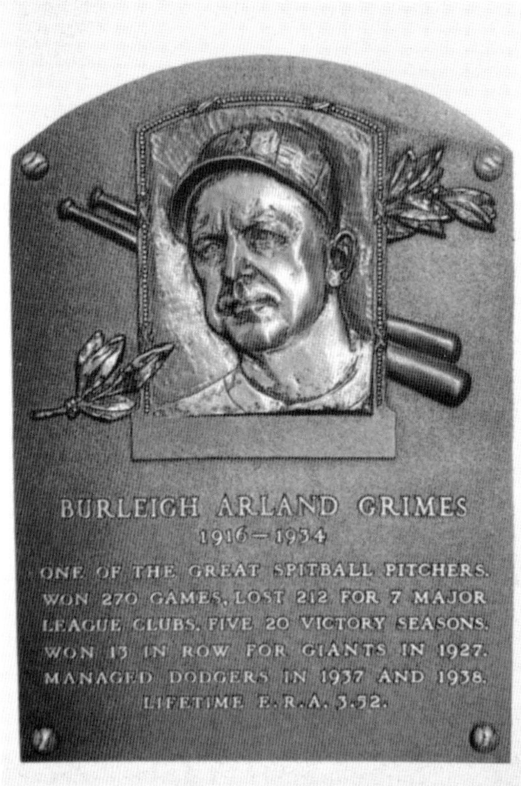

Entering the major leagues in 1916, Burleigh Grimes was a practitioner of the spitball. Ruled illegal in 1920, Grimes was grandfathered in and allowed to use the "spitter" for the remainder of his career, thus becoming the last pitcher to legally throw a spitball in major-league history. He had great success pitching with three National League teams in the 1920s and won 20 or more games five times. His two wins in the 1931 World Series helped the Cardinals win the championship. When St. Louis released the 40-year-old in the spring of 1934, the Yankees signed him as a reliever. Grimes joined a team that had nine future hall of famers in uniform. He earned the victory in his first game with New York for his 270th and final career win. Grimes was elected in 1964.

Branch Rickey said of Lou Gehrig, "His playing ability took second place to his sportsmanship; for Lou Gehrig was genuinely a nice guy . . . truly a gentle man. For many years he played in the shadow of Ruth, the phantom star, eternally the crown prince, never the king. In a lesser man, resentment would have been routine; but Lou Gehrig was not that kind of man."

"BABE RUTH" GHERIG.

It began in 1920 when he was 17 years old, and a century later, Henry Louis Gehrig remains inexorably linked to George Herman Ruth. Gehrig's Commerce High School team was in Wrigley Field playing in what the *Chicago Tribune* called the "High School World Series." Gehrig iced the game with a ninth-inning grand slam onto Sheffield Avenue: "A blow which any big leaguer would have been proud. . . .Walloped by a boy who hasn't yet started to shave."

A right halfback at Columbia on a football scholarship, he switched to the line, playing both guard and tackle. Then came the 1923 baseball season, his first. A first baseman and outfielder, he was asked to fill Columbia's pitching gap in February. By early May, sportswriter Hugh Fullerton tabbed him "another Babe Ruth," and Lou Gehrig, once tabbed the "Babe Ruth of High School," was now also known as "the Babe Ruth of Colleges." He signed with the Yankees on April 30, 1923.

Lou Gehrig and Mel Ott are pictured here before the 1936 World Series. As great as Gehrig was during the season, he was better in the seven World Series he played, increasing his batting average by .020 points. His slugging was also .099 higher. When Babe Ruth hit his 700th career home run in 1934, the closest player to him was Gehrig with 323, followed by Jimmie Foxx (248) and Ott (197). Both Foxx and Ott surpassed 500, while Gehrig was abruptly cut short in 1939, finishing his career with 493.

How good was Lou Gehrig? His lifetime OPS of 1.080 ranks him third all-time. He owns three of the top-six seasonal RBI totals in history, and in five seasons, he compiled 400-plus total bases. Only six other players in history have recorded more than one 400-plus total base seasons. Six times he recorded 200 hits and 100 walks in a season; his closest rival did it four times. He is one of only 10 players to win his league's Triple Crown and one of four to win the MLB Triple Crown. Among the game's top-three players in World Series production, he is the most dominant, most valuable, most productive first baseman of all time. The "Iron Horse" held his 2,130 consecutive-games-played record for over a half-century. His No. 4 was retired in 1939, and he was the first player in baseball to receive that honor.

On May 2, 1939, Lou Gehrig benched himself because he felt he was hurting the team. A little over a month later, he was diagnosed with amyotrophic lateral sclerosis (ALS), the disease that today bears his name. On Lou Gehrig Day, through tears, Gehrig delivered one of the most iconic speeches in sports history. The "luckiest man on the face of the earth" chronicled why it was so, among them: "I have never received anything but kindness and encouragement from you fans . . . a wonderful mother-in-law who takes sides with you in squabbles with her own daughter . . . a father and a mother who work all their lives so you can have an education and build your body—it's a blessing." He closed with his highest tribute: "When you have a wife who has been a tower of strength and shown more courage than you dreamed existed—that's the finest I know. . . . I might have been given a bad break but I've got an awful lot to live for." (Above, Leslie Jones Collection, Boston Public Library.)

Sixteen years to the day that he replaced Wally Pipp at first base, Lou Gehrig died at home. Babe and Claire Ruth were among the first to arrive and offer condolences. A century later, Gehrig's legacy endures. In 1995, hall-of-famer Cal Ripken broke Lou's record for consecutive games played, an event that brought positive attention back to MLB following the strike in 1994. In March 2012, Pete Frates, a former captain of the Boston College baseball team, was diagnosed with ALS. Intoning Gehrig, he spearheaded the "Ice Bucket Challenge," which raised over $220 million dedicated to ALS research. This led to "a grassroots effort," said Pete Frates's mother, Nancy, "by patients and families who were affected by this disease who found it to be unacceptable that there was not a day to honor Lou Gehrig, and made it happen." Frates passed in 2019, and in 2021, MLB designated June 2 as Lou Gehrig Day; it is celebrated every year throughout baseball.

The impact of the thunderous energy created by these two megastars echoes across the decades, manifested in bronze statues dedicated in May 2022 at Magnolia's Katy Ballpark at the Silos in Waco, Texas. Sculptor Scott Rodgers's website explains, "The purpose . . . to honor the history of Waco . . . these two men . . . the game of baseball, and bring people together. As folks sit with Babe and Lou . . . a sense of community is fostered . . . these sculptures are meant to be approachable. Two of baseball's greats chilling, having a good time, waiting for their turn at the plate. As both men were bigger than life . . . in real life, these monuments of Babe and Lou were sculpted a bit larger than life." The sculptures commemorate an April 1929 visit to Waco by New York, who beat the Cubs 13-3. Ruth doubled, and Gherig homered in the contest.

3

Joltin' Joe, Leading Man

Arriving in New York in 1936 with Hollywood good looks, Giuseppe Paolo "Joe" DiMaggio, the "Italian prodigy," was touted as "another Ty Cobb, Babe Ruth, and Tris Speaker." By 1939, he was recognized as the best player in baseball and did so overcoming the stereotypes and prejudices that beset so many immigrants. Noel Busch wrote in *Life* magazine, describing DiMaggio as "a tall thin Italian youth equipped with slick black hair and squirrel teeth. Although he spoke Italian first." He continued, "Joe, now twenty-four, speaks English without an accent and is otherwise well adapted to most U.S. mores. Instead of olive oil or smelly bear grease, he keeps his hair slick with water. He never reeks of garlic and prefers chicken chow mein to spaghetti." Joseph Paul DiMaggio, the "Yankee Clipper," reigned over the Yankees' most successful era and was a New York icon for seven decades. (Leslie Jones Collection, Boston Public Library.)

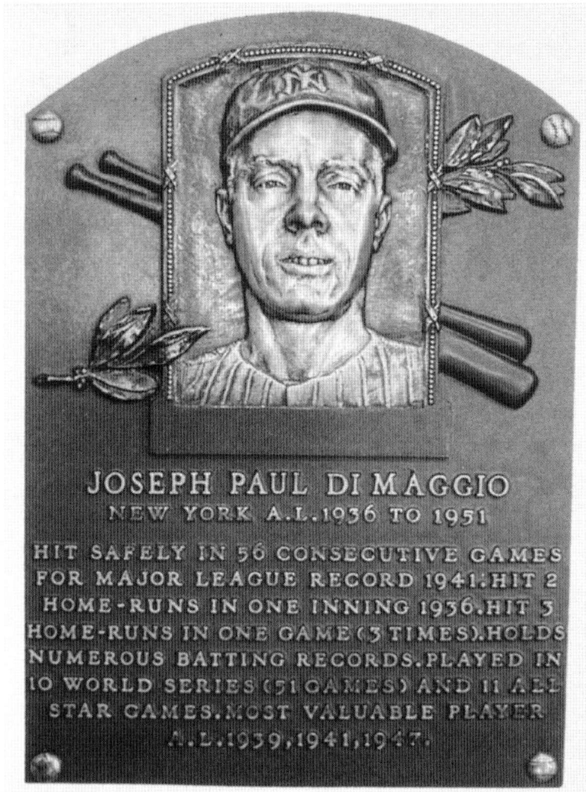

In 1933, Joe DiMaggio went from the sandlots of San Francisco to the Pacific Coast League and, in his first year of professional baseball, hit .340 with 169 RBI. Along the way, he set a record, hitting in 61 consecutive games. He once said that reaching the World Series was "the difference between taking the winter off or having to get a job." DiMaggio retired as the game's most prodigious winner, a nine-time champion of the world. He was elected in 1955.

The highly touted Joe DiMaggio arrived for his first spring training in St Petersburg. "I guess I'll like New York," he told Stuart Cameron of the *Brooklyn Times Union* and, "No, thinking of big league crowds doesn't bother me. . . . I just like to play baseball." Gehrig, jumping the bat, stated, "With that DiMaggio rifling the ball ahead of me, it will be like the old days of Murderers' Row."

New York sports columnist Bill Corum brought together Babe Ruth and Joe DiMaggio for their first formal introduction in January 1938 at the Friars Club Testimonial Dinner. DiMaggio was recognized as the Most Outstanding Athlete of 1937. A week later, the Baseball Writers Association honored DiMaggio as the Player of the Year. After pacing the AL in homers, he led the Yankees to their second Fall Classic win in a row.

In 1941, "Joltin' Joe" DiMaggio, the established icon, and Ted Williams, the rising star, became eternally linked. For DiMaggio, it began on May 15 and ended only after he hit in 56 consecutive games. For Williams, it culminated in Philadelphia, where his season ended with a .406 batting average. Three-quarters of a century later, DiMaggio's record still stands, and baseball still awaits its next .400 hitter. Both lost three playing years (1943–1945) to World War II.

Although his father, Giuseppe, was branded an "enemy alien" and his fishing boat was seized, Joe DiMaggio enlisted in the Army in February 1943. Assigned the "duty" of physical instructor, he spent a lot of time playing baseball. The Army stated he had a "defective attitude" toward military service; some speculate it was born of the mistreatment of his father. Joe was embarrassed by his assignment and requested a combat assignment but was denied. He was discharged in September 1945.

In spring training 1951, nineteen-year-old Mickey Mantle of Commerce, Oklahoma, hit .403 with a bushel of home runs. On opening day, he was playing right field and batting third. Joe DiMaggio was playing center field and hitting fourth. Mantle was wearing No. 6, a clear indication the Yankee brass considered him the "next great Yankee." Babe wore No. 3, Gehrig wore No. 4, and DiMaggio wore No. 5. DiMaggio retired following the 1951 season with his ninth World Series ring.

In January 1954, the marriage of Joe DiMaggio and Marylyn Monroe electrified the country. It would last but a year for their lives could simply not be reconciled. Deeply in love, DiMaggio remained devoted to Monroe until her death and beyond. In 1961, she accompanied him to spring training in St. Petersburg, and when she died the following year, he took care of all the funeral arrangements. For 20 years, Joe had roses delivered to Marilyn's grave three times a week.

Joe DiMaggio became a pop culture icon, fueled by his wedding to Marilyn Monroe, as a spokesperson for Mr. Coffee, and being mentioned in a dozen songs, with one asking, "Where have you gone, Joe DiMaggio? Our nation turns its lonely eyes to you." He lived out his days introduced as "the greatest living baseball player," making his last appearance at Yankee Stadium in September 1998, with Phil Rizzuto presenting him with World Series replacement rings, which had been stolen.

Twenty-two-year-old second baseman Joe "Flash" Gordon attended his first Yankee training camp in 1937, and although starter Tony Lazzeri knew he was looking at his eventual replacement, Lazzeri was gracious and professional enough to give Gordon extensive instruction, both offensively and defensively. Gordon spent that entire season with New York's top farm club and became the Yankees' starting second baseman in 1938. The rookie impressed right from the start, setting a record for American League second basemen with 25 home runs and playing exceptional defense. Offensively, he led the team in the 1938 World Series as New York captured yet another championship. Gordon became a perennial MVP candidate, nine-time All-Star, and five-time world champion. He won the 1942 MVP award over Ted Williams, who had won the offensive Triple Crown. He was elected in 2009.

"We're not afraid of DiMaggio . . . the man we fear is Gordon," said Dodgers manager Leo Durocher before the 1941 World Series. Truer words were never spoken, as Flash Gordon's performance in that year's Fall Classic is the stuff of legends. He batted .500; hit a double, a triple, and a home run; had five runs batted in; and walked seven times in the Yankee victory. Manager Joe McCarthy called him "the greatest all-around player I ever saw."

Considered one of the best bunters of his time, Phil Rizzuto led the major leagues in sacrifice hits for four consecutive seasons (1949–1952). A scrappy player, the diminutive shortstop (five foot, six inches and 150 pounds) was a huge cog in the Yankee machine, winning the American League's MVP award in 1950 after finishing runner-up to Ted Williams in 1949. Casey Stengel, who managed Rizzuto from 1949 through 1956, said that he was "the best shortstop he ever saw play."

Affectionately known as "Scooter," Phil Rizzuto was loved by generations of Yankee fans. Serving the team for 53 seasons as a shortstop and broadcaster, he was a part of nine pennants and seven world championships on the field and another dozen pennants and six world championships in the booth. The Brooklyn-born son of Italian immigrants was signed as an amateur free agent in 1937 and tabbed with his nickname by teammate Billy Hitchcock in 1939 while playing for the franchise's Kansas City farm club. The following year, Rizzuto was named the *Sporting News* Minor League Player of the Year, and in 1941, manager Joe McCarthy replaced longtime starting shortstop Frank Crosetti with Rizzuto. The longest-serving broadcaster in Yankee history, Scooter directly touched more Yankee fans than anyone who has ever donned the pinstripes. He was elected in 1994.

After retiring as a player late in the 1956 season, Phil Rizzuto (left) embarked upon a Yankee broadcasting career that would last four decades. His friendly, folksy manner immediately endeared him to the fans and was exhibited with his signature phrase, "Holy Cow," and his penchant for calling opponents and friends alike "Huckleberry." His Brooklyn Dodger counterpart, Pee Wee Reese (right), followed him into the booth as well, covering the *Game of the Week* for both CBS and NBC.

Prior to a game at Yankee Stadium, Phil Rizzuto is mingling with young members of his fan club. He became a fan favorite early on, and Joe DiMaggio would later say, "People loved to watch me play baseball, but Phil Rizzuto, they just loved." When Rizzuto arrived to ostensibly replace the very popular Frank Crosetti, many Yankee veterans worked to squeeze him out of time in the batting cage until DiMaggio intervened and said simply, "Let the kid hit." (Boston Public Library.)

Phil Rizzuto rocked a whole new generation of fans with his one-minute play-by-play in rock singer Meat Loaf's smash 1978 hit "Paradise by the Dashboard Light." Rizzuto simulated a baseball broadcast where a player is rounding the bases trying to score, a metaphor for a teenage romantic encounter in a parked car. Meat Loaf asked him to tour with him; however, he declined, saying, "Cora [Scooter's wife] would kill me."

When Paul Waner, more affectionately known as "Big Poison," arrived at Yankee Stadium in late 1944, his hall-of-fame credentials were already cemented in stone. The right fielder, who had spent his prime in Pittsburgh, won an MVP award in 1927 and had amassed over 3,000 hits. By 1941, however, he started moving from team to team as a part-time player and was released by the Dodgers on September 1, 1944. Waner was elected in 1952.

Signed by the Yankees the same day he was released by Brooklyn, Paul Waner, general manager Ed Barrow believed, could still provide a productive bat off the bench, which he did later that day at Yankee Stadium. He delivered a pinch-hit single, the last of his 3,152 career hits. He remained with the team for the duration of the season and came back the following spring before being released on May 6, 1945.

Although executive Larry MacPhail was bombastic, abrasive, and opinionated, he was also an innovative, creative, and well-respected baseball pioneer. In 1933, more than a decade before he joined the Yankees, he became general manager and top executive of the Cincinnati Reds. In 1935, MacPhail had lights installed at Crosley Field, and night baseball began. Moving on to Brooklyn in 1938, he became the Dodgers' executive vice president and general manager. He was elected in 1978.

The 52-year-old Larry MacPhail resigned from the Dodgers in 1942 to enlist in the military during World War II. After his discharge in early 1945, he purchased one-third of the Yankees franchise and became general manager. He hired Bucky Harris as field manager in 1947, and the team immediately returned to world-championship form. MacPhail, keeping a promise he made to his wife, retired following the victory and sold his interest in the team.

While Yogi Berra had outstanding hitting potential from early on in his pro career, management had doubts about his defensive ability as a catcher. When Casey Stengel was hired to manage after the 1948 season, he assigned former Yankee catcher Bill Dickey to work with Berra one-on-one, which produced terrific results. His fine defensive work and handling of pitchers proved a significant factor in his perennial All-Star selections, three MVP awards, 14 pennants, and 10 world championships. He was elected in 1972.

By 1950, Yankee catcher Yogi Berra could have stepped out of a Norman Rockwell painting or been a character created for *The Jack Benny Show*. There seemed to be no end to his "Yogi-isms" Among them were "Nobody goes there anymore—it's too crowded," "I'd give my right arm to be ambidextrous," The future ain't what it used to be," and "I never said most of the things I said." While much about him inspired laughter, his baseball accomplishments inspired awe. When Berra stepped on the field, he was deadly serious, ferociously competitive, and dedicated to one thing: winning. Despite his unathletic appearance, he displayed exceptional skills in many phases of the game. His famous nickname came from childhood friends who saw a movie featuring a turban-wearing snake charmer whom they thought looked like young Lorenzo Pietro Berra. They never dreamed that the World War II veteran of the Normandy invasion would become a national treasure known forevermore and simply as "Yogi."

One evening in 1947 over dinner and "a lot of scotch," Yankee owner Dan Topping and Red Sox owner Tom Yawkey agreed on a straight-up trade, Joe DiMaggio for Ted Williams. The next morning, Yawkey awoke with buyer's remorse and phoned Topping, telling him he would need to throw in the rookie outfielder Yogi Berra. In what would have been one of baseball's biggest blockbuster trades, Yogi was the deal breaker.

Yogi Berra first met Babe Ruth in St. Louis in June 1948. "I was really nervous," he recalled when "I went up and asked him if I could take a picture with him." By the end of his career, he surpassed the Babe in Yankee world championships, World Series games played, and World Series hits. In 1998, Yogi joined Ruth when he, too, was honored with a museum celebrating his life.

Phil Rizzuto lights Yogi Berra's cigar as they celebrate the birth of Yogi's second son. Upon Yogi's death, Yankee broadcaster Michael Kay, through tears, revealed a story about the pair. Rizzuto spent his last years in an assisted living facility, and every day Yogi visited, "They played cards . . . and he would hold his hand until he fell asleep. That's who Yogi was," said Kay, "every day . . . because he knew Phil was scared and sick."

The Yankees honored their star catcher with Yogi Berra Day at the stadium before a game on September 19, 1959. In the 35-minute ceremony, Yogi and his family were presented with 59 gifts, including a state-of-the-art color television. When Casey Stengel spoke, he said Berra was the greatest player he ever managed aside from Joe DiMaggio, who was also in attendance.

Joe Torre eulogized his friend. "All the stats," he said, "three MVPs, most World Series rings, managed both the Mets and Yankees to the World Series. But he was so much more than that. No matter what you read, it wasn't enough to find out what Lawrence Peter Berra was all about." Yogi became the most-treasured elder statesman of the Yankee family, and when all is said and done, he may well be the most-beloved Yankee of all time.

In 1946, the Yankees finished a distant third in the American League standings. That September, Stanley "Bucky" Harris began working for the team in an executive capacity, and in November, Larry MacPhail appointed him field manager for 1947. The 50-year-old Harris had already managed 20 seasons with five major-league teams. Joe DiMaggio once said, "If you can't play for Bucky, you don't belong in the major leagues." He was elected in 1975.

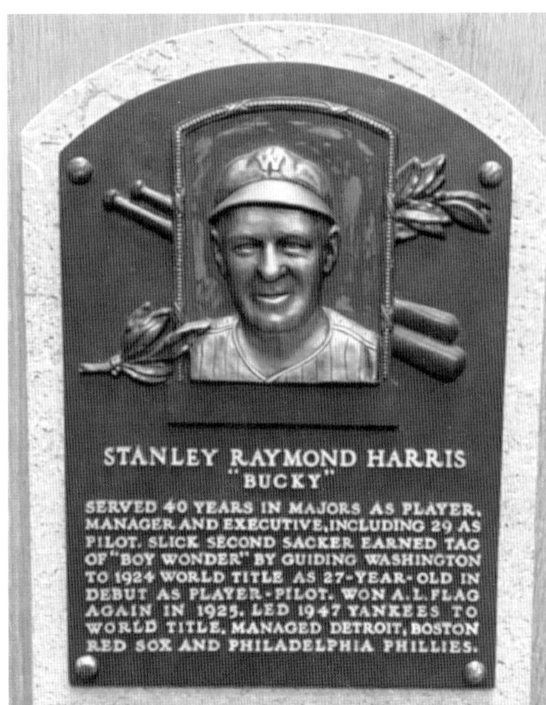

In 1924, twenty-seven-year-old Bucky Harris was hired to both manage and play second base for Washington. He led them to two consecutive World Series appearances, winning the world championship in 1924. Some 23 years later, his managerial talents were exactly what the Yankees, needed as they won the pennant and defeated the Brooklyn Dodgers in the 1947 World Series. Harris was replaced by Casey Stengel after the 1948 season.

Low-key executive George Weiss was happy to work behind the scenes and remain out of the spotlight while his shrewd moves helped build numerous Yankee world championships in his nearly three decades with the organization. Jacob Ruppert had been impressed with the way Weiss, a Yale graduate, ran Baltimore's minor-league team and hired him to head the newly created New York Yankee farm system in 1932. Weiss was elected in 1971.

When Larry MacPhail sold his share of the team to Dan Topping and Del Webb in 1947, they promoted Weiss to Yankee general manager. Weiss had overseen the signing and development of Joe DiMaggio, Phil Rizzuto, Joe Gordon, and Yogi Berra. He hired Casey Stengel as manager after the 1948 season, propelling the team into an era of unparalleled success. The Yankees won the World Series seven times over the next 10 seasons.

The only team in Major League Baseball history to win more than three world championships in a row are the New York Yankees. They have done it twice: 1936–1939 and 1949–1953, and George Weiss was a driving force behind both. Weiss worked from a distance and rarely met with players except for the team's top stars. Few could argue with this approach, as Weiss was named the *Sporting News* Executive of the Year on four occasions.

Hoping to hold off the surging Red Sox, in August 1949 the first-place Yankees acquired National League slugger Johnny Mize for $40,000. Mize, a perennial MVP candidate and nine-time All-Star, had hit 91 home runs over the previous two seasons. He remains the only player in major-league history to hit more than 50 home runs (51) while striking out fewer than 50 times (42) in the same season, accomplishing the feat in 1947. Upon joining New York, the 36 year old had a lofty .320 lifetime batting average, and his 315 home runs was sixth on the all-time list. Six weeks after becoming a Yankee, Mize appeared in the first of his five World Series with the team. "The Big Cat" was the batting star of the 1952 World Series victory, hitting, .400 with three home runs and six RBI. Mize was elected in 1981.

Behind a sometimes comical, even clownish, exterior, "Casey" Stengel possessed a brilliant baseball mind and exceptional leadership skills. Despite his unusual manner of speaking, often referred to as "Stengelese," most came to view him as "crazy like a fox." Born in Kansas City in 1890, Charley Stengel earned the nickname "KC" in a poker game during his rookie year; the name later evolved to "Casey." Debuting as an outfielder with Brooklyn in 1912, he developed a reputation as a rather eccentric individual but also a fine hitter, good defensive player, and speedy base runner. Playing with the New York Giants in the 1923 World Series, he hit the first World Series homer at Yankee Stadium. Hired as Yankee manager after the 1948 season, his managerial acumen and talented rosters produced historical results. In his 12 years at the Yankee helm, they averaged 96 wins per season, for an astounding winning percentage of .623, while capturing 10 pennants and seven World Series.

Hired two days after the 1948 World Series, Stengel was skewered by many in the press. Jimmy Powers of the *New York Post* called him "a clown" with poor judgment. The *Syracuse Post*'s Whitney Martin opined that Stengel's predecessor Bucky Harris had "done a fine job with a team that was disintegrating like a crumb cake." Although having never met him, Joe DiMaggio was present at the press conference to endorse Stengel's hiring.

Having just piloted the Oakland Oaks to the Pacific Coast League championship did not assuage the fact that Stengel's nine years managing in Brooklyn and Boston were awful. He had one winning season (77-75) and an overall record of 581-742. However, Charley Peet of the *Binghamton Press* said that "the demanding, exciting" Stengel would "put a little pep and color in the Yankees and the staid stadium." Peet was right, and with "pep and color," the team captured the 1949 pennant and World Series.

Testifying before a senate committee hearing on baseball's antitrust status, Stengel was asked a question by Tennessee senator Estes Kefauver. Stengel responded in classic "Stengelese," rife with meandering, colorful verbiage containing mixed metaphors, non sequiturs, fractured syntax, and his own peculiar style of double talk, which brought down the house. Kefauver followed up with, "What are your thoughts on that, Mr. Mantle?" To which Mickey Mantle replied, "I agree with Casey."

Casey Stengel and Ted Williams entered the hall of fame together in 1966. Williams spoke first and said, "I'm awfully glad to be with him on his big day. I also know I'll lose a dear friend if I don't stop talking. . . . I'm eating into his time, and that is unforgivable." In 1970, the Yankees retired his No. 37 and honored him with a plaque in Monument Park.

4

The "Mantle" is Passed

In January 1951, Casey Stengel wrote in his *New York Daily News* column that the 19-year-old shortstop prospect had "a chance to stick" with the 1951 Yankee team. On March 2, Stengel began the job of "converting him . . . to an outfielder." By March's last day, the *Daily News* was touting him as "faster than Cobb . . . the best switch-hitter ever . . . more powerful . . . than Ted Williams." In fact, he is "so great that Joe DiMaggio is ready to cede center field to him right now." And he had yet to play a game at Yankee Stadium. When he retired in 1968, he had hit more home runs than Williams and played in two more World Series than DiMaggio. Over a half-century after he left the game, Mickey Mantle remains "the best switch-hitter ever" and one of baseball's most-beloved figures of all time. He was elected in 1974.

His on-field accomplishments stand on their own, and in Bob Costa's eulogy, he encapsulated the totality of Mickey Mantle. In his waning days "he got love from America. . . . Love for the humanity and the sweetness that was always there; mixed with all the pain that racked his body and soul." He came to "accept and appreciate the difference between a role model and a hero. The first he often was not, the second he will always be."

Ted Williams, Yogi Berra, and Mickey Mantle are shown at the 1960 All-Star Game in Kansas City. Berra's favorite Mickey Mantle tale is when he called all the pitching signs from center field because "he wanted to see how good he was." Ted Williams said of Mantle, "He had the most natural ability of any player that ever played," and he was "the most humble man I ever met in sports."

In mid-July 1951, the Yankees sent Mickey Mantle to the Kansas City Blues, their AAA team, with instructions to manager George Selkirk (above) to play him in center field. He struggled when he arrived and called his dad, "Mutt" Mantle, revealing to him his doubts about whether he was "cut out" to be a big leaguer. Mutt drove to Kansas City. According to Mickey's recollection decades later, "He walked right past me and started packing my things. . . . 'I'm taking you home . . . you can work with me in the mines. I thought I raised a man not a coward.' . . . He had tears in his eyes and it tore me up. . . . It took me about 30 minutes to talk him into letting me have another chance." Mickey returned to New York in late August and was issued the No. 7. "The rest is history," said Mickey, and what a history it was.

In 1961, Mickey Mantle and Roger Maris were on pace to break Babe Ruth's 60-homer mark. An injury sidelined "Mick" in mid-September, and in true Mantle fashion and a manifestation of the fact, he was such an outstanding teammate, he became Maris's number-one fan. On October 1, 1961, Maris surpassed the Babe. On October 4, sixty-one years later, New York Yankee outfielder Aaron Judge broke Maris's record. (Gary Hershman.)

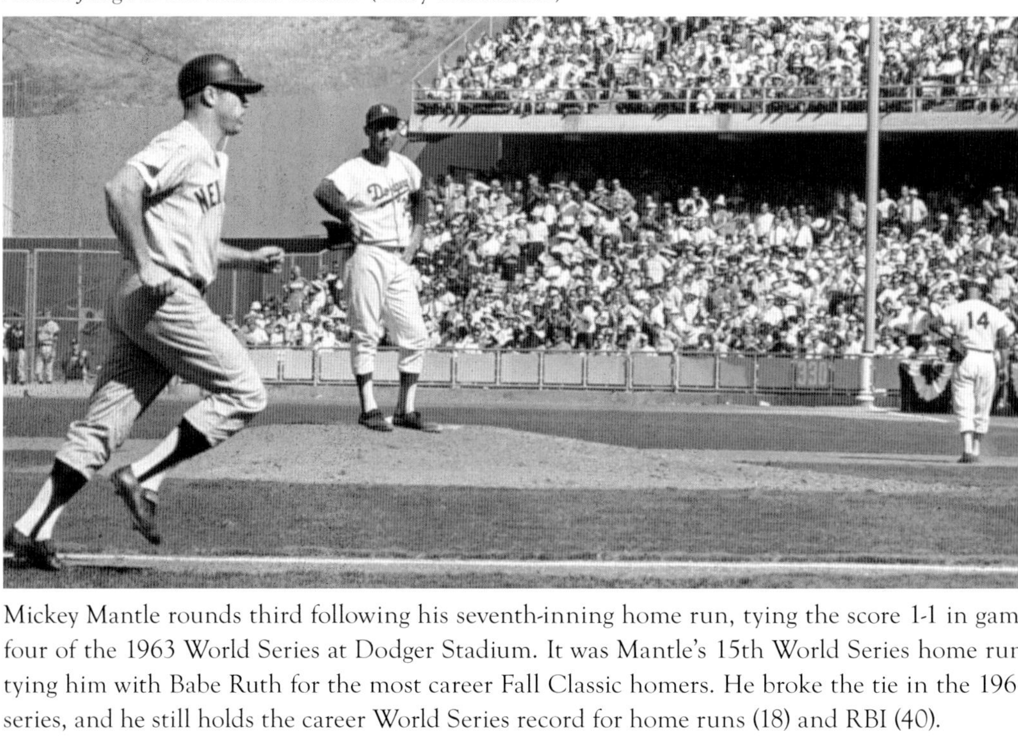

Mickey Mantle rounds third following his seventh-inning home run, tying the score 1-1 in game four of the 1963 World Series at Dodger Stadium. It was Mantle's 15th World Series home run, tying him with Babe Ruth for the most career Fall Classic homers. He broke the tie in the 1964 series, and he still holds the career World Series record for home runs (18) and RBI (40).

This photograph inspired a poem written by Mickey Mantle Jr. following his father's death: "Can I touch your face, Can I hold your hand, Can I give you a hug again and again, Can I say I love you, you're also my friend, My Father." In January 1994, Mickey Sr. checked into the Betty Ford Clinic seeking help to halt 43 years of heavy drinking that had seriously damaged his liver. He was inundated with letters. "I didn't realize until I started getting those letters," Mickey Sr. told Bob Costas in a poignant, emotional interview, "What I did mean to some people . . . it really helped." He received a liver transplant in July 1995, after which he openly spoke of his flaws and failings, endearing himself to millions. He closed the interview with Costas by saying, "I hope they say, he turned out all right . . . I'm proud that I named my son 'Mickey' . . . that'd be nice."

A 10-time National League All-Star, Enos "Country" Slaughter was acquired for the 1954 season by Yankee general manager George Weiss. In his first season in the Bronx, Slaughter made 30 appearances in the outfield and batted .355 in 43 pinch-hit at bats. Sent to Kansas City in 1955, he returned from the A's in 1956 and contributed to three consecutive AL pennants and World Series championships in 1956 and 1958. He was elected in 1985.

An intense competitor who would do virtually anything to win, right fielder Enos Slaughter was a pivotal figure on two Cardinal World Series championship teams. The *New York Times* once wrote, "On the ball field he is perpetual motion itself." His "Mad Dash" from first in game seven of the 1946 World Series against Boston scored the series winning run and etched his name into baseball folklore. His No. 9 was retired by the Cardinals in 1996.

Lee MacPhail joined the Yankees in 1946 as head of their top minor-league team, Kansas City of the American Association. Serving as director of player personnel from 1949 to 1958, he oversaw a farm system that produced players who led the Yankees to nine American League pennants and seven world championships. He became Baltimore's general manager in 1958 but returned to New York as Yankee general manager from 1967 to 1973. He was elected in 1998.

While Lee MacPhail (left) had a dramatically different personality than his hall of fame father, Larry (right), both shared a passion for baseball. Lee's accomplishments are even more impressive than those of his noteworthy dad. A key component of 20 years of Yankee dominance, MacPhail said he was proud to have been present when 17-year-old Mickey Mantle signed his first contract. Lee and Larry are the only father and son tandem in the hall of fame.

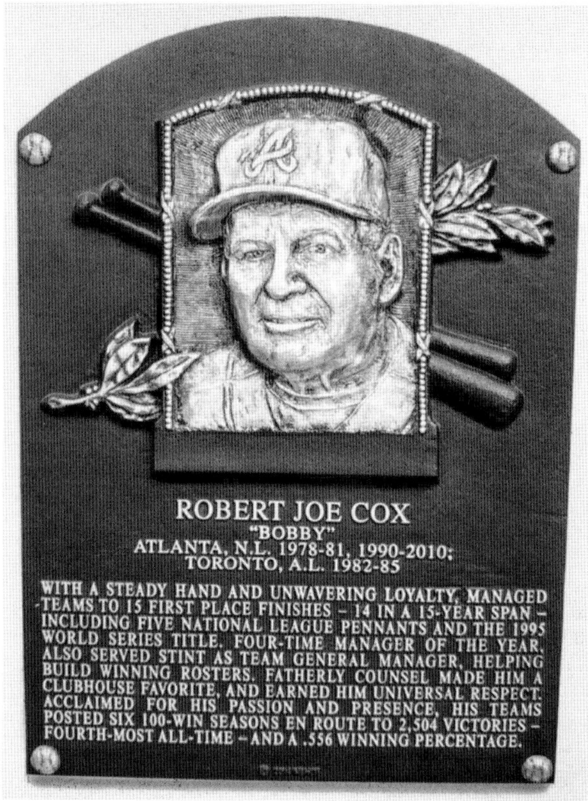

His claim to fame is managing the Atlanta Braves to 15 division championships, five National League pennants, a World Series title in 1995, and winning four Manager of the Year awards. However, Bobby Cox's path to the hall of fame began in Yankee Stadium where he laid the foundation for his major-league career as a Yankee infielder in 1968 and 1969. Traded from the Braves organization to New York in December 1967, he was named the starting third baseman the following spring. He was elected in 2014.

The Oklahoma native was thrilled to be a teammate of Mickey Mantle, who was playing his final season. On June 3, 1968, Cox and Mantle, who was playing first base, achieved the rare feat of being involved in turning a triple play. Cox's playing career concluded with New York in 1969, and he began managing in the minors. Cox served as a coach under Billy Martin on the 1977 Yankees.

Twelve days after the Yankees won their third World Series in 1928, Edward Charles Ford was born in Manhattan. When he was five years old, his family moved to Queens to a neighborhood of Irish, Polish, and Italian immigrants. There he became a loyal Yankee fan and idolized Joe DiMaggio. Ford's first manager was former Yankee pitcher Lefty Gomez, who gave the blond-haired Ford the nickname "Whitey." The 5-foot, 10-inch, 170-pound lefty joined Gomez in the hall of fame in 1974.

A pitcher and first baseman, Ford pitched a 10-inning, two-hit shutout in a local championship game played at the Polo Grounds, creating a bidding war between the Red Sox, Yankees, and Giants. The war was won by the Yankees, and Ford signed for $7,000. What the Yankees did not know was that the talented southpaw would have signed for their initial offer of $2,000; his heart was always set on the Yankees.

Called up in July 1950, the 21-year-old Whitey Ford went 9-1, which included three three-hitters. With the Yankees ahead three games to none in the World Series, Ford said to broadcaster and future hall-of-famer Dizzy Dean "These Phillies are so easy I can see how you won so many games in the National League." Ford then won game four, completing the sweep—his first World Series win. Ford and Yogi Berra competed in 11 World Series together.

Following his rookie year, Whitey Ford enlisted in the Army and missed two seasons. Upon his return in 1953, he was relegated to the bullpen until his first appearance (which consisted of four innings, no runs, and three hits). Placed back in the rotation, he led the team with 18 wins and pitched the final game of the World Series and left it leading 3-1. After being tied in the top of the ninth, the Yankees won it in the bottom half, clinching their fifth-straight World Series.

By 1955, Whitey Ford (right) was one of the elite pitchers in baseball. He, along with Mickey Mantle (left) and Billy Martin (holding a beer bottle with Bob Grimm between them), had established a reputation for a fondness of the nightlife and off-field extracurricular activities as well. In a 2002 interview with Tim Russert, Ford began a story with "we were out having a few drinks." He paused and said, "It sounds like we were drinking all the time." "I think that's a given, Whitey" came the affable Russert's reply.

Whitey Ford won his only Cy Young Award in 1961. Instituted in 1956, the Cy Young Award was to reward the Most Valuable Pitcher. From 1956 through 1966, only one pitcher was selected throughout MLB. A strong case could be made for Whitey Ford winning the award outright in both 1956 and 1958, and there is no doubt he was the AL's best pitcher in both those years and perhaps 1959 and 1963 as well.

Ford's calm, cool demeanor under pressure led Yankee catcher Elston Howard to tab him "the Chairman of the Board." The ace of the Yankee staff for the better part of 15 years, Mickey Mantle said of him, "I don't care what the situation was or how high the stakes were; the bases could be loaded and the pennant riding on every pitch. It never bothered Whitey, he pitched his game, cool, crafty, nerves of steel."

Whitey Ford retired in 1967 with 236 wins, still the most in Yankee history, and he holds the World Series record for starts (22), innings pitched (146), wins (10), and strikeouts (94). The Yankees won 11 pennants and six World Series during Ford's tenure in the Bronx. Casey Stengel, who once described Ford as "quiet, egotistical, and witty," welcomed him and Mickey Mantle into the hall of fame. In 1987, his plaque was dedicated in Monument Park.

5

Mr. October Stirs New York

Reginald Martinez "Reggie" Jackson and the New York Yankees were made for each other, and by the time he arrived in the Bronx in 1977, his resume included an AL MVP award, a World Series MVP award, and three World Series rings. He spent five seasons in pinstripes and played in three more World Series, winning two of them, and added another World Series MVP. His electrifying play in the 1977 and 1978 series earned him the moniker "Mr. October." His five home runs in the 1977 Fall Classic set a new record that had been shared by Babe Ruth and Lou Gehrig. He played only five of his 21 seasons in New York, yet on his hall of fame plaque, he is appropriately wearing a Yankee cap, for on baseball's biggest stage, in baseball's biggest moments, he shined brightest with the Yankees.

While Reggie Jackson was with Oakland, the A's won five consecutive division titles, three straight AL pennants, and three straight World Series. In New York, he was part of four AL East titles, three pennants, and back-to-back world championships. His five years in California brought two AL West titles. The Yankees retired his No. 44 in 1993, and the A's followed in 2004 with Jackson's No. 9. He was only the 10th player to have his number retired by two teams. Jackson was elected in 1993.

Nobody who knew Yogi Berra did not have a favorite "Yogi story." Reggie Jackson's was being on the line with him at an Old-Timers' Game awaiting the national anthem. A video was playing on the scoreboard in remembrance of all Yankees who had passed away the previous year. As the names were scrolling, Berra nudged Jackson, "Hey, hey," he said to Reggie, "I hope I don't ever see my name up there." (Bryan Yablonsky.)

A 1964 graduate of Cheltenham High School in Pennsylvania, Reggie Jackson was bound for Arizona State University on a football scholarship and an agreement that he could "try out" for the baseball team. During his senior year in high school, he hit .553, threw two no-hitters, and once struck out 19 in a seven-inning game. He played halfback for the Sun Devils and made coach Bobby Winkles's baseball team. In 1966, he found himself replacing center fielder Rick Monday, who was the overall first pick in the first-ever draft of 1965. Monday signed with the Kansas City Athletics for $100,000. Jackson said replacing Monday was "like replacing the sun and the moon." Jackson was drafted by Kansas City the following year and signed for $80,000. Five-time Yankee world champ and Athletic scout Eddie Lopat was present for the signing.

Reggie Jackson plants a kiss on the cheek of winning pitcher Ron Guidry following the Yankees' win in the 1978 playoff game against the Red Sox. The teams finished tied for first in the AL East, and it was decided in one game at Fenway Park. Jackson's solo home run in the eighth inning provided the difference. The Yankees captured the 1978 World Series, and Guidry (25-3, 1.74 ERA) copped the Cy Young Award.

Jim "Catfish" Hunter had just turned 19 when he made his big-league debut with the Kansas City Athletics in May 1965. Two months later, as the Beatles performed their historic concert at Shea Stadium, Hunter made his first start in Yankee Stadium, a complete-game 4-3 win. The Athletics moved to Oakland in 1968 where "Catfish" became a superstar. From 1971 through 1974, he won 88 games, a Cy Young Award, and three-straight world championships.

After being embroiled in a breach of contract dispute over Athletics' owner Charles O. Finley's failure to make required insurance payments, Jim Hunter was declared a free agent by an arbitrator in mid-December 1974. Following MLB's first all-out bidding war for a true superstar, Hunter signed the most lucrative contract in major-league history: a five-year, $3.75 million deal. Hunter was introduced to the New York faithful at a press conference on New Year's Eve (above) and joined a Yankee team on the precipice of returning to their glory days. Catcher Thurman Munson was a key component of their resurgence. Hunter and Munson won three-straight pennants together and back-to-back World Series in 1977 and 1978. In August 1979, Munson perished in a plane crash, and Hunter retired at the season's end.

Jim Hunter had made it clear before the 1979 season that it would be his last despite the fact he was only 33 years old. On September 16, the Yankees celebrated "Catfish Hunter Day" at Yankee Stadium, and among the many wonderful gifts he received was this 5,000-pound elephant. Hunter retired to his farm before dying prematurely at the age of 53 due to complications from ALS, also known as Lou Gehrig's disease.

Rich "Goose" Gossage grew up a Yankee fan in Colorado and he played on nine teams in 22 seasons. "I absolutely loved every minute I played on every team, but putting on those Yankee pinstripes was really something special," he said. His years in New York were his best, and his teammate Rudy May perhaps explained why. "Hitters always have the fear," he said, "that one pitch might get away from him and they'll wind up DOA with a tag on their toe."

Rich "Goose" Gossage, with his imposing physical presence, penetrating scowl, and tremendous fastball, was the prototype for today's closers. One month after beating the Dodgers in the 1977 World Series, the Yankees upgraded their pitching staff by signing the 26-year-old Gossage as their new bullpen ace. Having established himself with both the White Sox and Pittsburgh, he arrived in New York a three-time All-Star, which, coupled with his signing of an extremely lucrative contract, created high expectations for Gossage as he joined the world champion Yankees. He was so highly regarded that the Yankees made him the closer over Sparky Lyle, who, in 1977, became the first American League closer to win the Cy Young Award. On his way to becoming the second pitcher to reach 300 career saves, Gossage notched 151 saves, 42 wins, and four All-Star appearances in his six years in New York. He was elected in 2008.

Rich Gossage met all expectations in his 1978 debut season in pinstripes. Recovering from a faulty start, he pitched 134 innings in 63 games, leading the league in saves (27), and he was once again an All-Star. He recorded a two-and-one-third-inning save in the playoff game with the Red Sox, a save in the pennant-clinching game against the Royals, and was on the mound to clinch the World Series against the Dodgers—the Yankees' first back-to-back world championship in 16 years.

Five years after making his debut as an outfielder with Cleveland in 1941, Bob Lemon was converted to a pitcher. Over the next decade, he was one of the finest pitchers in the American League, winning 20 or more games seven times. He was one of the Indians' top aces on the 1948 World Series champions and 1954 pennant-winning team, which won 111 games. He managed the Yankees for parts of four seasons. Lemon was elected in 1976.

Shortly after retiring in 1958, Bob Lemon began a long span of coaching and managing in both the major and minor leagues, joining the Yankees as their pitching coach in 1976. On July 25, 1978, he was named New York manager, replacing Billy Martin, and took a team that was 10 and a half games back to a World Series victory. The tables turned when Martin replaced Lemon in 1979 after he was let go by George Steinbrenner.

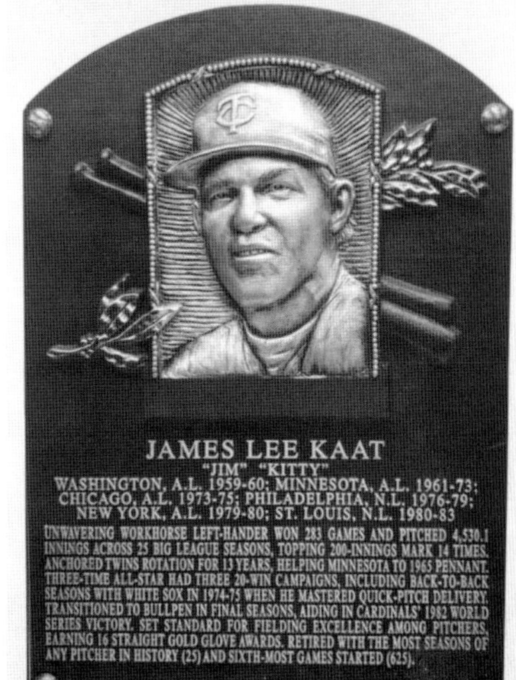

When the Yankees acquired 40-year-old lefty Jim Kaat from the Phillies in May 1979, he had amassed 254 victories over 21 seasons and had reached the 20-win plateau three times. However, the aging Kaat was transitioning from starting pitcher to middle reliever and, except for one starting assignment in 1979, made 39 appearances in that role. After four appearances in April 1980, New York traded Kaat to St. Louis. He was elected in 2022.

In St. Louis, Kaat won a World Series title in 1982 before retiring several months later. He won 16 consecutive Gold Glove awards from 1962 to 1977 and is tied with hall of fame third baseman Brooks Robinson for second-most all-time, trailing only Greg Maddux, another hall of fame pitcher, who won it 18 times. Kaat joined the Yankees television broadcast team for the 1986 season and again from 1995 to 2006.

The first-place Yankees had a slim division lead over the defending American League champion Baltimore Orioles and wanted to add an experienced veteran to the pitching staff. On August 14, 1980, they acquired star Gaylord Perry, notorious for "doctoring" the baseball, from the Texas Rangers. He made his first appearance two days later with a victory over the rival Orioles. Perry was elected in 1991.

"Will the real old guy please stand up?" was the greeting from Ron Guidry to the newly acquired 42-year-old Gaylord Perry as he sat in front of his locker talking to Luis Tiant. Perry won 20 or more games five times, amassed over 3,000 strikeouts, was the only pitcher to win a Cy Young Award in both leagues, and had also thrown a no-hitter. Perry is ninth all-time with 690 career starts, and his milestone 600th came in pinstripes.

In his seven full seasons in the Bronx, David Winfield's average year was 150 games, 26 homers, and 102 RBI. In 1981, his first as a Yankee, he led the team in hits, RBI, and OPS as they won the AL pennant. While in pinstripes, he won five Gold Gloves and five Silver Slugger awards and was consistently among the American League's most productive players. Missing all of 1989 with a back injury, he recovered and in 1992 had his career best year in Toronto, where he became a world champion.

Few athletes can claim the distinction of being drafted by multiple sports teams. Dave Winfield became the first in history to be selected by four. The six-foot, six-inch University of Minnesota star was drafted by the San Diego Padres (MLB), Minnesota Vikings (National Football League), and two pro basketball teams, the Atlanta Hawks (National Basketball Association) and Utah Stars (American Basketball Association). Winfield chose baseball and jumped directly to the major leagues where his exceptional athletic ability was obvious immediately, and he quickly proved himself to be a complete all-around player. Winfield's commitment to his community was also evident when he created a charitable foundation and donated game tickets to low-income fans. After several seasons as the top player on a mediocre Padres team, Winfield took advantage of free agency and in December 1980 signed a 10-year, $23 million contract with the Yankees, the richest contract in professional sports history. He was elected in 2001.

On opening day 1981 at Yankee Stadium, Dave Winfield batted third in yet another powerful Yankee lineup. He immediately began justifying his lofty contract, and when the players' strike began on June 12, his .324 average and 39 RBI were among the league leaders. Upon baseball's return in August, Winfield made his first of eight consecutive All-Star appearances in a Yankee uniform and helped lead New York to their fourth World Series in six years.

After spending 20 seasons with the National League Milwaukee/Atlanta Braves, knuckleballer Phil Niekro switched leagues, signing with the Yankees in January 1984. Though he would turn 45 years old by mid-season, Niekro reigned as the team's top starter by a considerable margin. He won his first four starts in pinstripes, and on July 4, he joined the exclusive 3,000 strikeout club. He was elected in 1997.

Phil Niekro was named to the All-Star team and compiled a 16-8 record, becoming the oldest pitcher to win 16 games in a season. In 1985, his final season with New York, he repeated the feat, winning 16 games again. His final game with the Yankees was on October 6, a complete-game shutout for his milestone 300th win. Ironically, during that historic game, Niekro threw only three knuckleballs, all to the last batter, who struck out swinging on the flutterball.

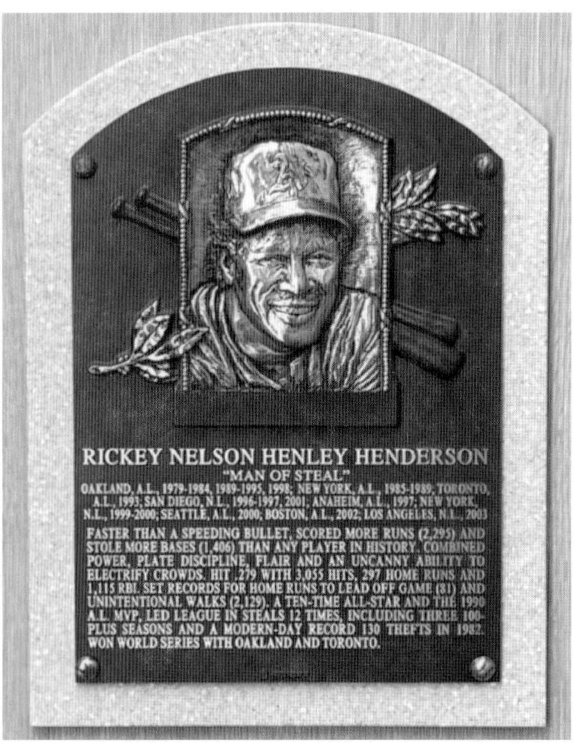

Few players in baseball possessed the skill set of Rickey Henderson. Accomplished in many phases of the game, the "Man of Steal" is largely remembered for his stolen base exploits, and his name is synonymous with his base-running expertise. Henderson surpassed hall-of-famer Lou Brock's stolen-base record in 1991 and continued to add to it for 12 more seasons. Henderson's career total of 1,406 is a record that may never be broken. He was elected in 2009.

Rickey Henderson established himself as a star in his six seasons with Oakland before being traded to the Yankees in December 1984. In a little less than five seasons in New York, he made four All-Star appearances. One of the game's true characters, he always spoke in the third person. "He was one of the best players that I ever played with and obviously the best leadoff hitter in baseball," said fellow hall-of-famer Dave Winfield.

From 1980 through 1991, Rickey Henderson led the AL in stolen bases every year except for 1987, when he was injured. The 1987 stolen-base champ was Harold Reynolds with 60. In classic Henderson style, he called Reynolds at the season's end. "Henderson here," he opened. "What's up?" said Reynolds, expecting congratulations. "Sixty stolen bases, you oughta be ashamed," said Henderson, "Rickey had 60 at the All-Star break." And he hung up, leaving Reynolds laughing.

On August 31, 1993, the second-place Yankees, who were closely trailing division-leading Toronto, acquired dominating closer Lee Smith. The imposing six-foot, five-inch, 250-pound pitcher had led the National League in saves the previous two seasons and was among the leaders at the time of the trade. Earlier in the 1993 season, Smith passed Jeff Reardon to become the all-time leader with his 359th save. At 35 years old, Smith was still extremely effective and allowed no hits in his first three Yankee appearances. A few weeks later, on September 17, he achieved a major milestone with his 400th career save against his former team, the Red Sox. In his eight appearances with New York, he did not allow an earned run. Smith held the record for career saves from 1993 to 2006, until Trevor Hoffman surpassed his total of 478. He was elected in 2019.

6

THE CAPTAIN AND THE SANDMAN

On June 5, 1992, the *New York Daily News* queried whether number-one draft pick Derek Jeter would choose the University of Michigan or the Yankees. On that same page, a headline read, "[Mariano] Rivera Gets Rave Reviews in 'A' Ball." Jeter, the 19-year-old top draft pick from Michigan, and Rivera, the 23-year-old non-drafted pitcher from Panama, met the following year in Greensboro, North Carolina. They made their MLB debuts six days apart and then cried together in a New Jersey restaurant three weeks later when they were sent back to Columbus. Yet, before it was all over, Jeter and Rivera would lead the Yankees back to an era of dominance they had not enjoyed in a half-century. For over 2,600 games, they were teammates, and no two Yankees captured and embodied the Yankee mystique, over an expanded span of excellence and superiority, better or longer than "the Captain" and "the Sandman."

Born in New Jersey in 1974, the Jeters moved to Kalamazoo, Michigan, when Derek was four. Every summer, he returned to New Jersey to visit his grandparents and their home, where he would play whiffle ball in grandma's backyard, pretending to be Dave Winfield. Many a trip was made to Yankee Stadium as well. In his teens, Derek decided he was going to be a ballplayer, vowing to his family they would one day watch him play in Tiger Stadium. Committed to playing at the University of Michigan, he was ranked *Baseball America*'s top prospect his senior year, and his coach, Don Zomer, let it be known to all he was a better person than a player. Before his career was over, he joined Winfield in the exclusive 3,000-hit club, and in 2020, he joined him among Cooperstown's bronzed immortals. And on June 7, 1996, his family watched him play in Tiger Stadium. (Below, photograph by Ron Antonelli.)

Scouting for the Houston Astros, hall of fame pitcher Hal Newhouser implored the team to draft Derek Jeter first overall in the 1992 draft. When the team made Phil Nevin its first choice, he resigned. Jeter fell to the sixth spot, much to the delight of the Yankees. Forsaking his scholarship to the University of Michigan, the Kalamazoo Central high schooler signed for over $700,000. The Minor League Player of the Year at triple-A in 1995, he was the American League Rookie of the Year in 1996.

Jeter made his MLB debut on May 29, 1995, in Seattle and four days later came to bat at Yankee Stadium for the first time. In an amusing twist, comedian Jerry Seinfeld announced him, imitating Bob Sheppard, the longtime voice of Yankee Stadium. Sheppard retired in 2007 after 56 years, and Jeter asked him to make a recording of his introduction, which was used at Yankee Stadium until Derek's retirement in 2014, four years after Sheppard passed away.

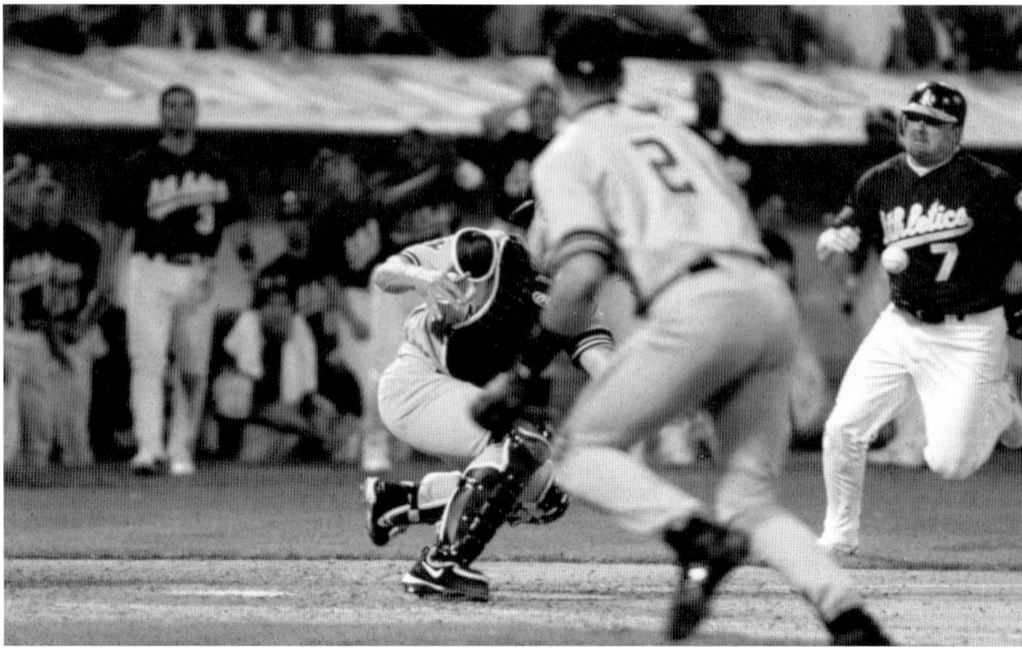

In October 2001, an iconic moment, which came to be known as "the Flip," provided the primary example of Derek Jeter's defensive acuity. It was game three of the AL Division Series in Oakland, with the Yankees down two games to none and facing elimination. Leading 1-0 with the A's Jeremy Giambi (No. 7) on first with two outs, a double down the line threatened to tie the score when right fielder Shane Spencer overthrew first baseman Tino Martinez. The errant throw was in foul territory when Jeter appeared from nowhere backing up the play and flipping the ball to Jorge Posada to nail Giambi at home, ending the inning and sealing the win. The Yankees went on to take the series. Jeter's hustle and grit on defense earned him five Gold Glove Awards. (Above, Linda Cataffo.)

In July 2011, Derek Jeter reached the 3,000-hit plateau with a home run. Tampa's first baseman Casey Kotchman recalled the moment. "On a single," he thought, "I'll have the chance to be the first one to shake his hand. But when he went in the seats, I had to just tip my cap." Always clutch and with a flair for the dramatic, Jeter's last career hit at Yankee Stadium was a walk-off single.

By the time he was 26, Derek Jeter had created a body of work and a mystique reminiscent of Joe DiMaggio. He captured his fourth World Series ring in 2000 when he became the first player to win an All-Star Game and World Series MVP in the same season—a distinction he still holds. Thousands of times, he passed under the sign of the DiMaggio quote thanking "the Good Lord for making me a Yankee," touching it every time he took the field.

Derek Jeter retired as the Yankees' all-time leader in hits (3,465), doubles, stolen bases, and games played. A 14-time All-Star, he is the only career Yankee to reach the 3,000-hit plateau. One vote shy of unanimous election, he made light of it in his induction speech. "I want to thank all the Baseball Writers Association, all but one of you." He closed by urging today's players to "take care of [the game], protect it . . . respect it. . . . Don't take . . . playing . . . it for granted."

Wade Boggs was regarded as one of the best pure hitters in baseball, prompting Ted Williams to say, "He may have the best hand-eye coordination of anyone I have ever seen." Incredibly disciplined, with a great batting eye and superior knowledge of the strike zone, Boggs produced seven consecutive 200-plus hit seasons. He posed such an offensive threat that he led the league in intentional walks for six consecutive seasons. He was elected in 2005.

Wade Boggs's work ethic and focus helped him win five American League batting titles, lead the league in on-base percentage five consecutive seasons, and become a 12-time All-Star. Boggs signed as a free agent with the Yankees in December 1992 and spent five seasons in the Bronx. In his first season in New York, he hit .302 and won a Silver Slugger Award.

Wade Boggs continued his offensive prowess after joining the Yankees while also dramatically improving his defense at third base. While wearing pinstripes, he won his only two Gold Glove Awards in 1994 and 1995. He appeared in four consecutive All-Star Games with the team and helped lead the "Bronx Bombers" to a world championship in 1996, its first since 1978. Boggs later became the first player to hit a home run for his 3,000th hit.

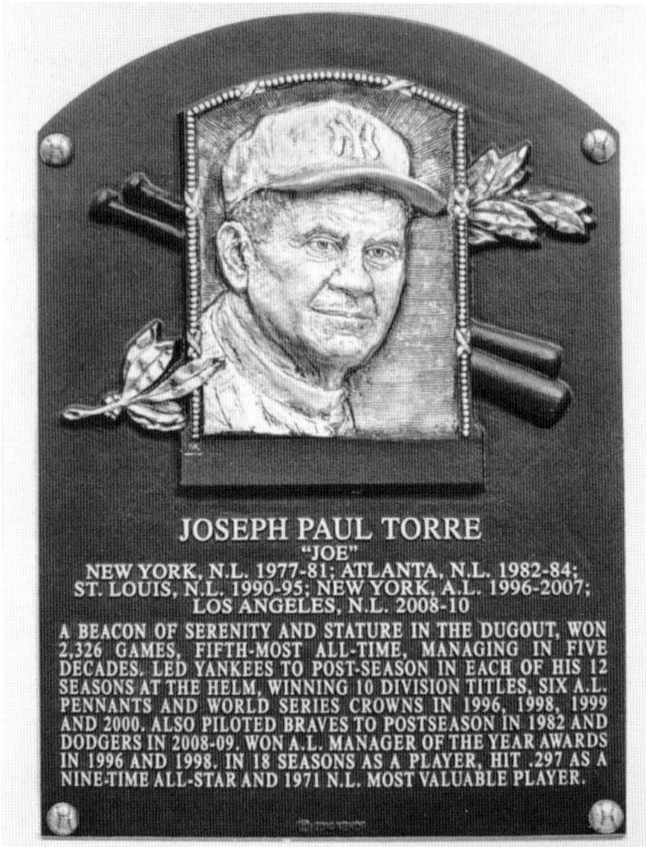

New York City native Joe Torre followed his brother Frank to the major leagues, making his debut in 1960 with the Milwaukee Braves. Torre had a tremendous 18-year playing career, splitting time between catching and first and third bases. After finishing runner-up in the Rookie of the Year voting in 1961, he captured a Gold Glove behind the plate in Milwaukee in 1965 (catching 148 games), an MVP award as the Cardinal's third baseman in 1971, and appeared on nine All-Star teams.

Joe Torre briefly served as player/manager for the Mets in 1977 before transitioning to full-time managing duties. Leaving the Mets following the 1981 season, he managed three years with the Braves in Atlanta and six with the Cardinals before becoming the Yankees skipper in 1996; a move that completely changed the trajectory of his career. Torre piloted in a new era in New York and yet another Yankee dynasty. He was elected in 2014.

In hiring Joe Torre, George Steinbrenner merged his managerial expertise and leadership skills with an extremely talented and well-balanced team. The *Daily News* said he possessed "a natural presence that commands respect." The World Series, which had eluded Torre for over three decades, was captured his first season in the Bronx as the Yankees won their first world championship in 18 years. Torre led his team to four World Series titles in his first five seasons.

A month after his induction into Cooperstown, the ultimate Yankee tribute was bestowed upon Joe Torre: a plaque in Yankee Stadium's Monument Park. He became the fourth Yankee manager to be so honored, joining Miller Huggins, Joe McCarthy, and Casey Stengel. Derek Jeter said of "Mr. T," "His demeanor, his style, rubbed off on players." The respect his natural presence commanded brought New York six pennants and four World Series championships in his 12 years at the Yankee helm.

Tim Raines made his mark early on as a speedy left fielder with the Montreal Expos. In 1981, he led the National League with 71 stolen bases and finished second in the Rookie of the Year voting. Raines is the only player in history to have at least 70 stolen bases for six consecutive seasons, with a career high of 90 in 1983. He played three season in New York and was elected in 2017.

Affectionately known as "Rock," the seven-time All-Star was acquired by New York in December 1995, beginning his three-season stint with the team. Though his tenure was often injury plagued, he stole his 800th base while in the Bronx. In 1996, Raines contributed to the first Yankees world championship in 18 years, and he won another ring with the team in 1998.

Just weeks removed from winning their third consecutive World Series, and 26th overall, the Yankees signed coveted free agent star pitcher Mike Mussina, one day before his 32nd birthday. Raised in a small Pennsylvania town, Mussina had reservations about signing with a team in the largest baseball market in America, but a phone call from Joe Torre convinced him it was a good fit for both him and the Yankees. Ironically, the small-town Mussina started almost 60 percent of his games on three of baseball's biggest stages: Camden Yards, Fenway Park, and Yankee Stadium. He made his debut with the Orioles in 1991 and garnered 147 wins in Baltimore. A five-time All-Star, "Moose" was also a perennial Cy Young Award candidate. In 1999, he finished second in Cy Young voting behind Pedro Martinez, who had one of the greatest seasons in history.

Joining an already impressive pitching corps, Mussina stepped right in and led the Yankee staff in earned run average (ERA) in 2001. On September 2 at Fenway Park, he flirted with history, giving up one hit, which came with him just one out away from a perfect game. His 17 regular season and two playoff wins aided the Yankees to the AL pennant and an appearance in the World Series, his first. He was elected in 2019.

Although a franchise pitcher most of his career, the 20-win milestone eluded him until his final season. In 2008, the 39-year-old posted a 20-9 record, becoming the oldest pitcher in history to reach the magic 20-win plateau for their first time. The victory, his 270th, came in the final game of his illustrious career. Since 1943, with the exception of Roger Clemens, no pitcher has won more games in the American League than Mike Mussina.

When Yankees longtime starting catcher Jorge Posada suffered a season-ending shoulder injury in 2008, the team acquired Ivan "Pudge" Rodriguez from Detroit. The 36-year-old veteran of 15 years was the premier catcher in baseball, a world champion, the owner of 13 Gold Glove Awards, a 14-time All-Star, and the American League MVP in 1999. Rodriguez led the majors in throwing out base stealers nine times, including six years in a row (1996–2001). Pudge arrived in New York with 2,584 career hits, 504 doubles, and a .302 batting average. His final home game in pinstripes was on September 21, 2008, the last game ever played in the original Yankee Stadium. The legend Johnny Bench once said about Rodriguez, "He was the complete catcher, incredibly durable and intimidating behind the plate but also a very good hitter." Rodriguez was elected in 2017.

The Yankees were seeking to continue their streak of seven consecutive American League East Division titles when they acquired 6-foot, 10-inch, left-handed ace Randy Johnson from Arizona. When "The Big Unit" arrived in January 2005, he was still a dominating power pitcher and had hurled a perfect game the previous season. In 17 seasons, Johnson had a resume of dominance, including five Cy Young Awards (four consecutively), two no-hitters, 10 All-Star appearances, nine strikeout titles, two 19 strikeout games in 1997, and a world championship and World Series co-MVP in 2001. He won 34 games over two seasons with the Yankees, including the 250th of his career as New York won division titles both years. He was traded back to Arizona in January 2007, and his 4,875 career strikeouts are second all-time, trailing only Nolan Ryan. Johnson was elected in 2015.

Raised in the tiny fishing village of Puerto Caimito, Panama, in a two-room house with no water or electricity, Mariano Rivera Giron espoused to be "the next Pele." He played baseball as well, using tree limbs for bats, gloves fashioned from milk cartons, and balls comprised of fishing nets wrapped in electrical tape. From these humble beginnings, he became the first player in the history of the game to be a unanimous selection for the hall of fame in 2019.

In the sugarcane fields with his grandfather, he learned to "bend his knees and swing the machete blade around his entire arm," a motion that became "his effortless, fluid pitching delivery." Rivera signed in 1990 for $2,000, a pair of shoes, and a new glove, beginning a five-year journey through the Yankee farm system that began in Tampa. He was left unprotected in the 1992 expansion draft, was almost traded in 1995, and ultimately ascended to heights that no player had ever been.

Mariano Rivera was so effective in the set-up role in 1996 that he placed third in the Cy Young Award voting. He also threw 14 1/3 innings (0.63 ERA) in the postseason as the Yankees captured their first World Series in 18 years. Throughout the year, he tinkered with a new pitch that emerged the following June. Known as "the Cutter," it became baseball's most famous pitch, of which the deeply religious Mariano said, "It is as if it dropped straight from the heavens."

A ferocious competitor, Mariano Rivera's focus was always on winning: "I don't just think of regular season; I think playoffs, World Series." His reputation for performing at his peak under pressure was cemented in the postseasons of 1998 and 1999. In 18 games, he hurled 25 1/3 innings, allowing zero runs with 20 strikeouts. He retired the MLB leader in most World Series saves (11), most league championship series saves (13), and most division series saves (18).

The new millennium brought with it "walk up songs" for batters and entry songs for closers. Yankee Stadium scoreboard producer Michael Bonner utilized the song "Enter Sandman" by the rock band Metallica as Mariano Rivera took his long, slow walk to the mound. The song's haunting opening chords signaled impending doom for opposing hitters. The association with the song and the band was mutually beneficial to Rivera and Metallica, seen together at Yankee Stadium.

When Mariano Rivera joined the Yankees in 1995, he was issued No. 42, and in 1997, when MLB retired it throughout the game in perpetuity, 13 players wearing it were allowed to continue to do so. In 2004, he was the only one left. "Every day, I was thankful to God . . . and . . . Jackie," he said. Rachel Robinson, who often praised Rivera for "his values, grace, and principles," said that "he represented her late husband as well as anybody could have."

In 2019, Pres. Donald Trump presented Mariano Rivera with the Presidential Medal of Freedom, America's highest civilian award. Rivera told a heartwarming story of how he asked Greensboro teammates Tim Cooper and Bob Deller to teach him English. "By the end of the year I could communicate . . . and I was the happiest man in baseball. I realized I could do something for others . . . teach them that learning English is the first thing we should do. . . . I'm proud to be an American."

The embodiment of humility, dignity, respect, and grace, Mariano Rivera opened his induction speech by thanking "my good Lord and savior Jesus Christ for giving me the talent to play baseball." Repeating, several times, throughout his 25-minute speech, "You don't get here alone," he effusively expressed his love and gratitude to all who played a hand in his growth and development as a player and a man, calling his wife, Clara, whom he met in elementary school, "the pillar, the backbone of our family."

Mariano Rivera, Andy Pettitte, Derek Jeter, and Jorge Posada were referred to as the Yankees' "Core Four." Playing together two years in Columbus, the four made their big-league debuts in 1995 and were part of seven Yankee pennants and five world championships. Pettitte and Jeter both came to the mound to remove Rivera, or "Mo," from his last game. In his induction speech, Rivera said simply, "I tried to carry the pinstripes the best I could." The "best" of the hall of fame tandem of Mariano Rivera and Derek Jeter was exceptional. Joining previous Yankee duos of Ruth and Gehrig and Mantle and Ford, the duo returned to the Bronx the Yankee tradition of dominance and dynasty. Combined, these six men are party to 33 Yankee pennants and 22 world championships. Mantle and Ford were the most prolific and Ruth and Gehrig were the most dominant, but none did it longer than "the Captain" and "the Sandman."